Endo

MW00699600

"The quality of life is not merely about what happens to you but how you respond to it. Tiran shows us how to intentionally triumph over tragedy. Learning and being inspired from someone who chose to be resilient amid great tragedy is a priceless gift!"
—Bishop Dale Bronner,
Word of Faith Family Worship

"Tiran's story is one of incredible strength and resilience. He has faced both emotional pain and physical challenges on his journey, and yet he has found a way to give others hope and provide them a path to overcome their adversity. His story is nothing short of inspiring for anyone facing challenges and struggles in their life!"
—Andy Henriquez, Professional Speaker,
Founder of Mater Storyteller Academy

"Tiran's story is one of inspiration and motivation. He lived his life without letting the challenges stop him, even when he lost his wife and was missing a leg! Reading about how bravely this man faced everything from physical pain, emotional heartbreak, to mental exhaustion left me feeling empowered in my own abilities and ready to make positive changes in my life."
—Malorie Bailey, Entrepreneur, Public Figure

"As an amputee who's had to face tremendous adversity myself, I was deeply impacted by Tiran's journey. His obstacles are different than what most others face, but when they're met with the faith, love, and service to others that Tiran demonstrated, any challenge can be turned into a tremendous opportunity for growth. And that message is universal and much needed in today's world."

—Zach Gowen, Professional Wrestler, Speaker, and American Ninja Warrior

CHOOSING
resilience

ALL THINGS WORK TOGETHER FOR GOOD

TIRAN JACKSON

FREILING
PUBLISHING

Melissa,

I appreciate you hearing my story
& hope that it touches & inspires you.

Tiran Jackson   7/21/2023

Written by Christen M. Jeschke

Published by Freiling Publishing,
a division of Freiling Agency, LLC.

P.O. Box 1264
Warrenton, VA 20188

www.FreilingPublishing.com

PB ISBN: 978-1-956267-40-2
eBook ISBN: 978-1-956267-41-9

Printed in the United States of America

Dedication

This book is dedicated to my beautiful Maleka.
We miss you every day.

Contents

Part III: Resilience Resolve

Acknowledgments

This book is for anyone who has ever loved and lost, especially those who found themselves in a difficult place after something unexpected happened. The adversity we face can be the key to unlocking our strength and resilience within, helping us by making other challenges in life seem easier with every step taken on the journey.

This book is also dedicated to those that knew Maleka personally or were impacted by her death. I also want to dedicate it to all those who have been there for me, both in my personal life and professionally, who have supported me during the trauma. Specifically, I would like to thank my mom, Shirley Jackson, brother-in-law/sister, Gregory & ReVonda Hawkins, my closest friends who are brothers to me, Roy Dawson and Christerpher Jones, our TSU Family, my I.P.P.P brothers, and Maleka's father, Malvin Grimes. I am very grateful for all of these people in my life, but they provided thoughts, support, and prayers during the most challenging time of my life.

Lastly, with love from my immediate family, I have been able to tell this story and share it with the world. They've provided me support when times were tough. My wife Kaye deserves an enormous level of credit for her encouragement throughout everything—she's helped provide motivation for me to complete this book because of her love and how much belief she has in me. In addition, our boys, Jaylen and Cameron, have given support in ways beyond what I would have imagined.

"Our whole lives

were ahead of us—

and then she was gone."

Prologue

Picture Perfect

I draped my arm gently around my wife, Maleka, as our boat gracefully skimmed through the crystal clear aquamarine water surrounding the beautiful Exuma shoreline. The sun glinted off the gentle waves lapping against the catamaran. The weather, like the day before us, seemed perfect.

I cradled Maleka against me, grateful for the opportunity to celebrate fifteen years of marriage and excited for our future together. Our trip to the Bahamas was a chance to reconnect and strengthen our vibrant marriage, enjoying time away from life's distractions and drawing closer together. I loved this woman with everything inside of me and was so blessed to share this beautiful place with her, making new memories and looking forward to a long future together.

I scanned the sights on the horizon as other passengers on the boat chattered excitedly around us. If there were picture-perfect moments that could last forever, this was one that I would cherish. Our whole lives were ahead of us—and then she was gone.

Part I

Maleka

"Climbing out of a stuck state was a choice, and I would make it, one step at a time."

1

Don't Stay Stuck

"Vonda! Vonda! Wait!"

My sister ReVonda walked home from the bus stop after school and passed right by the yard of the small home daycare where my mom deposited me while she went to work. I ran to the fence at my daycare as fast as my tiny legs could carry me. My arms outstretched toward my sister, I pleaded for her to take me with her, my eyes wide brimming with unshed tears.

I was relentless as I followed her along the fence line, calling to her and crying out for her to set me free from the boundaries of the play yard. She would try to ignore me and continue with her friends, but she was my fiercest protector and greatest champion even then. If I needed her, she would gather me in her arms and take me home. She hated to see me confined and would scoop me up and take me with her, even as her friends laughed and teased her for doing it.

My father, mother, sister, and I lived in a small house on an acre of land in a two-stoplight town called Cherokee, Alabama, nestled near the

Alabama-Mississippi state line. Although our home was in Cherokee, the larger nearby town of Florence, Alabama, was where we lived our lives. This was where I went to school, played sports, and participated in activities. Florence was the type of town you either spent your whole life in or left and never looked back. I wanted to leave and never return.

My sister, ReVonda, would get the chance to escape long before I did. She was born to my mother ten years before I came along. My father wasn't her biological dad, but he raised her as his own. Despite our decade age gap, ReVonda and I were always close.

If you asked her, ReVonda would say that I was spoiled as a child. The truth is that when she left for college by the time I was eight or so, I did become like an only child. With my sister gone, I became more isolated, learning to live life on my own, playing video games, listening to music, and generally entertaining myself in the absence of a sibling.

Even though I was inherently introverted, I was a reasonably popular child. I realized at a young age that I was very smart and instinctively knew that if I used the gift of my intelligence wisely, it could be my ticket out of my small town, and I wanted out. I watched with envy as I saw my sister experiencing life beyond Cherokee, and I desperately wanted to follow in her footsteps. When she left for college, I longed to follow her. If pleading with her worked as well as it did in my daycare days, I would have begged her to take me. Her life at college was a vastly different world from the one surrounding me. As ReVonda gained new experiences, my desire to one day achieve similar experiences grew exponentially. She chased after her dreams, and I wanted the chance to pursue mine.

My mother recognized my intelligence but never really pushed me in school. My father was a laborer who barely achieved a high school diploma, so academics was not an area that he emphasized. My parents may not have been content in the life that they had, but they weren't trying to change it either. This didn't sit well with me. I wanted to do more, achieve more, grow more, live more. I longed to break free of the town's ties in whatever way I could and exceed my potential.

When I was in elementary school, a teacher identified me as potentially gifted and arranged for me to take an IQ test, verifying her hunch. The knowledge that someone else thought I was brilliant gave me confidence in my school work. Straight A's came naturally to me, so I pushed myself to achieve bigger goals. Whether through athletics, academics, or special groups or events such as chess tournaments, I was determined to get the hell out of my town and make a better life for myself.

All around me, I saw people who were stuck. They were stuck in what was comfortable, stuck in a demanding but predictable life—stuck under the influence of the same friends and mired in generations of unhealthy behaviors. My own parents were stuck.

My dad was an alcoholic addicted to booze and nicotine, smoking one to two packs of cigarettes every day. His life consisted of working and then drinking himself into an incoherent stupor. He was too engaged in his destructive pattern to engage in my life, rarely attending any of my athletic or academic functions. My mom tried to make up for it by showing up for me, but she locked herself in a pattern of fussing at my father's failures without really making any effort to fix things for herself. They both existed in a dysfunctional atmosphere without ever trying to dig themselves out. Somewhere they inadvertently made a choice—a choice to slowly crumble instead of building a more vital, solid life for themselves. I knew that I didn't want to follow this path, yet I would be mired in it myself if I didn't choose wisely.

My dad didn't talk a lot, but when he did, it was a drunken ramble spoken at me but not to me. He did not talk about anything that reached or related to me. He had a bit of a stutter, which made it challenging to start conversations with people, but when he drank, that pause that he had in his speech disappeared, and he would talk endlessly. When he and my mom spent time with friends, it was an atmosphere of accepting life as it was—a group of people complaining about where they were without ever trying to move beyond it. I despised this complacency. I didn't understand how a life of hard labor with low pay or few possibilities could ever be fulfilling. I wanted more for myself. I didn't want to look back on my life discontent with unreached dreams about places beyond the bounds of Florence, Alabama.

As a teen, I was split between two different groups of people—two separate and polarizing atmospheres. The athletes were the popular crowd. They boosted my status and esteem in school as I ran track and played football and basketball. Most of my friends in this group barely picked up a book, yet they were the cool kids. I could hang with the cool kids, but I had discovered that a more significant part of my identity lay in my nerd side. I knew that my intelligence could take me places, so I applied myself to compete at math and chess competitions, ranking consistently in the top of the state for these achievements. Whereas my athletic friends seemed content to play sports and mouth off about the game they just won, my academic friends were constantly growing themselves and their abilities. I admired this.

I knew that I had two paths before me. The one that would take me places was the one that pushed me past my comfort zone of accomplishments. I was good at sports, but my intelligence would be the ticket to take me out of that town if I was willing to pursue the gifts that God had naturally given me.

In my gifted classes, I met a boy named Curtis Franks. We weren't super close or anything, but he matched me academically, and we often paired off against each other in chess competitions. Occasionally, I was invited to play at his house or have dinner with his family. This opened my eyes to a new world beyond what I knew. My parents were probably lower middle class, but I had everything I needed and was grateful that I never lacked food, clothing, or shelter. I didn't have anything extravagant beyond that. Neither did most of the families that I was related to or knew. I don't know what Curtis's parents did for a living, but his house was nice—really nice. I had often watched TV families with awe, noting that there was life or belongings beyond my simple existence, but the Franks family showed me that more wasn't just on TV; it was attainable. Just like the families on TV, Curtis's family seemed to love and enjoy each other's company, all sitting down together for family dinners or talking about their day. It was an eye-opening experience to see that not all families had to deal with the fussing, fighting, and drinking that were constantly present in my chaotic home. This contrast sharpened my focus on removing myself from small-town life ties and reaching new heights somewhere else where I could grow and achieve instead of being mired in a life with no future beyond a paycheck-to-paycheck existence.

I decided that being stuck was not an option for my life. I was going to push, stretch, attain, and grab every opportunity in my reach to make a better life for myself. I would grow beyond this town and blaze a path broad enough for anyone to follow in my footsteps. If sports were the route to higher education, I would play harder and work more diligently than any of the other children. If academics were my ticket out, I would apply for every camp and scholarship that I could find. I fought to excel at chess, math competitions, or anything else that could give me an advantage. Frequently, this meant that I encountered resistance. My "cool" friends would tell me that I spoke too intelligently and would tease me for being such a nerd. My nerd friends would wonder why I spent so much time with the jocks. I didn't let either side bother me. I knew that if I followed my gifts, I would reap the rewards and find a path to success. Climbing out of a stuck state was a choice, and I would make it, one step at a time.

"Too often, people waste
time trying to make average
skills excellent instead of
maximizing the skills
in which they are naturally
talented or gifted."

2

Meant for More

Quivering with nervous energy, I channeled my anxiety into excitement as I began a presentation in front of the other summer campers. I spoke confidently, injecting a bit of my personality into each word and idea that I brought forward. Typically more quiet or shy, a certainty and boldness in my knowledge of the subject propelled me forward. With each phrase uttered, I grew more self-assured. When I ended my presentation, the other participants clapped, smiling approvingly.

That camp, the summer between my eighth grade and freshman years, was a game-changer for me. I knew that I wanted to get away from my small-town life, but this experience solidified that I had the skill and a pathway to achieve it. My guidance counselor recognized my aptitude for academics and recommended attending a leadership camp at a university in Montgomery, Alabama. Provided with a scholarship, I jumped at my first chance to be on my own, stay in dorms, and acclimate to an environment of strangers. I was excited about the opportunity and immediately connected and thrived. The other children in the camp were intelligent and voracious learners like me, and we bonded over shared learning and interests.

Throughout camp, we worked in teams to prepare for our final presentation. My group was composed of six children, but only two of us volunteered to speak onstage. I bravely stepped forward to explain my part. The feeling of presenting was exhilarating. It gave me confidence that I hadn't otherwise known I possessed. It also reinforced the idea that I needed to push myself beyond what I knew and to grow in spaces and environments that stimulated my thoughts, allowing me to advance my abilities. That experience solidified that I needed to reach for more and follow an attainable pathway to do it. Since I qualified for a camp scholarship, I knew I could eventually earn a college scholarship if I worked hard enough.

This confidence nurtured and reinforced the belief that I was meant for more. No longer focused solely on the dream of leaving my small town, I realized that I had the talents and abilities to be someone who achieved beyond what I had initially ever thought possible. I soaked up all the leadership knowledge that I learned from that camp and determined that although what I knew in Alabama was familiar and safe, I would accomplish far more if I reached beyond that and pushed myself to new challenges and opportunities.

My high school guidance counselor, Ms. Thelma Robinson, recognized that I was gifted in math and science, and she scoured for options to help me advance in that. She would call me up and tell me, "Tiran, I want you to apply for this STEM camp."

Whenever I traveled to a camp or program outside my area, my eyes opened a little bit wider to the array of possibilities that lay before me. Scattered around various historically black colleges were Science Technology Engineering and Mathematics (STEM) programs that had scholarships available to kids like me. Each camp that I attended gave me confidence and a certainty that I was pursuing the right path. I still played high school football and basketball and ran track, but my focus narrowed even more to academic achievement. By the time I had reached eleventh grade, I knew that I wanted to become a mechanical engineer and to attend a university with solid STEM-based programming.

Too often, people waste time trying to make average skills excellent instead of maximizing the skills in which they are naturally talented or gifted. I was good at football, but not great. I was good at track but not collegiate athletics bound. If I pursued that path to college, it wouldn't lead anywhere lasting. I was smart, was an excellent test taker, and had a great GPA, so I began to apply for as many academic scholarships as possible. I knew that my parents couldn't afford for me to follow the opportunities I wanted, so I knew that scholarships were the answer. With the encouragement of my guidance counselor, I applied to various schools and scholarship programs inside and outside the state of Alabama.

Various scholarship opportunities started to roll in, primarily for partial scholarships. A decade prior, my sister ReVonda attended Tennessee State University (TSU). I visited her there when she was enrolled, and that visit was one of the first tastes that I had of life outside of Cherokee. It whetted my appetite for more, and now, as a high school senior, I had a chance to revisit it. As I toured the picturesque Nashville campus, I instantly fell in love. I knew that this was the university that I wanted to attend. An opportunity for a full engineering scholarship solidified my choice.

I didn't understand all of the details at the time, but I soon learned that their scholarships were assigned based on a six-week summer program. All of the scholarship candidates attended this six-week program. To receive a full scholarship, I would have to perform in the top third of all students in the program. I worked hard, and I earned my full scholarship at the end of the summer. I would be attending the engineering program at TSU. My dreams for more had nurtured a desire that had grown into a plan through hard work and focus. This plan pursued opened a broader pathway for future success.

"We can fight our hardest against what we can't control, or we can take charge by choosing a path of resilience."

3

Life Is Not Fair

School had always been easy for me, but as I moved into my course of study, it grew increasingly more difficult. The general education classes that I had breezed through didn't challenge me in the same way that my engineering classes did. For the first time in my life, I found myself having to work hard to stay on top of my grades within the classes that comprised my major.

As the end of my freshman year came to a close, I completed several interviews to secure a summer internship. I finally settled on an internship with Nissan in Murfreesboro, Tennessee. Since my sister lived in Nashville, Tennessee, I planned to live with her over the summer while commuting to Nissan. Everything seemed to be lined up, and I had received a letter from Nissan confirming that I would be starting there at the end of the school semester.

The week before finals, I received a call that derailed all my plans. Nissan had decided that they didn't want me for the summer internship. I didn't want to go back to Alabama to stay with my parents for the summer, so I would either need to find a job to stay with my sister, or I would have to hurry to find an internship that would accept last-minute applicants. This left me scrambling to make a course of action.

At TSU, the dean of the college of engineering and the dean of mechanical engineering was a professor named Dr. Decatur B. Rogers. Dr. Rogers had overseen the six-week summer program that gave me my scholarship to TSU, and as a result, he was familiar with me. The pre-college engineering camps and programs were valuable recruiting platforms to attract new students each summer. TSU students usually staffed these programs while earning scholarships to supervise the younger students and instruct them in the programs.

When my internship with Nissan fell through, I spoke with Dr. Rogers and asked him if he had anything available for me. He assured me that he did and that I could work as his assistant or second in command, acting as a liaison between him and the various programs that he oversaw. This meant that I would stay on campus for the summer and work for him.

There were six different programs that six program managers ran. I was tasked with communicating between the programs and Dr. Rogers. In part, I acted as a buffer who managed any problems or issues that arose within the programs to avoid Dr. Rogers' involvement in anything that would unnecessarily consume his time.

I thought this job would be a great solution to my internship problem. I could stay on campus during the summer, attend classes, keep my scholarship, and help supervise the programs. I would be able to practice leadership, gain experience, and be directly mentored by the dean of my program. This seemed to be an ideal solution.

Dr. Rogers was gruff, stern, and had high standards. He would let people know if he wasn't satisfied with their standard of work in a somewhat intimidating way. A few of us students worked for him together and often needed access to the copy machine. The copier in Dr. Rogers' office was assigned a code to make a count and cost assignment per print. Those of us who had the code were supposed to use it sparingly and only for department-based projects. One of the girls working with us consistently displayed a shocking lack of integrity and would freely give out the code to her friends or classmates. Her poor judgment created a huge problem as soon Dr. Rogers realized that the copier use he was being charged for was excessive.

He was not pleased. His office noted that paper was rapidly disappearing, and the copier code was being used dishonestly by unauthorized users. He took the girl aside and asked her who was responsible for the issue. Uncomfortable under his scrutiny, she lied and said, "Tiran. I saw him giving out the code."

Dr. Rogers was furious and pulled me aside to set me straight. "I didn't do it," I countered. "I have no reason to lie if it was me."

He chose not to trust me and fired me as he believed I was lying to him, choosing the girl's version of events over mine.

I was hurt that he didn't believe me and angry that I was being unfairly accused. I confronted the girl who was responsible. Chagrined, she told me, "I didn't want to get fired, so I am covering my own ass."

This did not sit well with me at all. I remained on campus to take summer classes, but I was stripped of all of my duties and responsibilities with the program. This fostered some bitterness inside me toward Dr. Rogers. Whenever I was in his proximity, or he was in mine, we didn't speak, a heated tension emanating from both sides.

I couldn't avoid him forever, though. When the spring of my sophomore year rolled around, I was required to retake his thermodynamics class, a necessary evil to graduate. I did not relish having to sit in Dr. Rogers' class all semester while I roiled inside with anger over the injustice of the situation.

On the first day in his class, Dr. Rogers explained that each student would be assigned a grade based on two different factors at the end of the semester. The first factor was our performance in his class on tests, assignments, projects, etc. The second factor was a subjective assessment based on what the professor thought we had mastered during the course. One score would be based on what we earned, and he would give the other at his absolute discretion. I had never heard of a grading scale like this, and given the mutual animosity between Dr. Rogers and me, I felt uneasy about it.

However, I was determined that I wouldn't let Dr. Rogers hold me back in life or in that class. If I had to endure his class, I would excel at it and prove him wrong. In each lecture, I sat in the front row and made sure that I knew the material far better than any other student. If he asked the students a question, my hand was the first one raised. I actively engaged in any discussion that I could. As far as I could see, I went above and beyond doing everything required of me. My grades reflected my hard work, and I was eager to finish the semester strong.

Our final in that class was a presentation in front of the other professors in the department. I watched as Dr. Rogers lobbed easy questions at the students who were presenting. When it was my turn, his demeanor shifted, and instead of soft questions, he made it his goal to embarrass me in front of the class.

When we were dismissed, my classmates commented, "Why was Dr. Rogers going after you so hard? He didn't do that to anyone else. How did you get on his bad side?"

His targeting of me felt personal, and my feelings weren't assuaged when my grade from his class was released. My earned grade in his class was eighty-seven percent, which was a hard-earned B, but the grade that Dr. Rogers assigned to me was a D. This grade of D in a core class meant that I would have to retake the entire course. To say that I was pissed was an understatement. I was heated.

Desperate to change my grade and angry at the injustice of the situation, I did what any strong, self-respecting, fiercely independent college student would do—I recruited my mom to appeal to him. She met with Dr. Rogers, and instead of standing up for me, she folded like a piece of paper. He told her that I didn't perform up to the standard of what he expected of me. She didn't fight for me or push back. It was a complex, messy situation because he was the person responsible for my scholarship, and if I went up against him, I could lose everything.

The whole experience was incredibly humbling. I had to put my anger and ego aside to even walk into his classroom the following year. In that situation, I had no control. He had power over my scholarship and over my program, and he was the only professor who taught that class. I could not control his actions, but I did my best to control my attitude and actions.

Oddly enough, I retook his class as the teacher's assistant (TA). Dr. Rogers issued a stern warning to me as his TA: "You'd better get everything right in my class, because I am going to be using your answers as the key for the other students, and if anything is incorrect, that is going to be on you."

He would mock me in class in front of the other students: "Tiran didn't like his grade, so he brought his momma in to complain," or "Your TA didn't perform up to standard, so he's taking the class with the rest of you."

Sometimes it just got to be too much. However, we begrudgingly developed gradual mutual respect as the semester progressed. If I had been arrogant before, I was now compliant and worked even harder to meet his approval.

Later conversations would reveal that Dr. Rogers had found out that I was wrongly accused in the situation with the printer but that he had to hold someone accountable. Although he never truly acknowledged ownership in the situation, he would later tell me, "You have a lot of potential, and I see that. Part of my job is to prepare you when you go out into the world as an engineer. You need to understand that life isn't going to be as clear and straightforward as you want it to be. I felt that I needed to humble you and teach you that it is not enough to know the material, but you need to have the right attitude. In the world of engineering, you are going to have to work twice as hard and be twice as good as everyone else."

To be clear, I completely disagree with his logic. I don't think that injustice is necessary for character building. However, I did come to peace with the events that had transpired, and they gave me confidence that even when life seemed unfair, I could navigate difficulties with grace and learn from them.

I also learned that I wasn't the only student singled out over the years and given a lower grade than what our work earned. Apparently, this was something that he did to shape certain students that he saw with potential. Knowing that didn't reassure me, but it gave me insight into his methodology.

Over time, Dr. Rogers became one of my favorite professors, and I gleaned so much from his teaching and his guidance. Had I held on to bitterness or resentment, I would not have been able to do this. I let go of the things I couldn't control and learned from the experience, gaining wisdom within imperfect circumstances. He taught me professionalism and work ethic, instilling a foundation of solid work skills. Our dynamic was unusual, but in the end, I did gain value from it from a professional standpoint.

He often quoted 1 Corinthians 13:11 (NIV): "When I was a child, I talked like a child, I thought like a child, I reasoned like a child. When I became a man, I put the ways of childhood behind me." As part of this, he would lecture about the timeline of our lives. He would say that other people's decisions mostly shaped us until the age of eighteen, whether parents, teachers, or other adult leaders. He believed that the periods on our life timeline of eighteen to twenty-four were incredibly critical, as this was when we began to make decisions on our own—some of which could affect the entire trajectory of our lives. He encouraged us not to rush through this stage, making brash or careless choices, instead of using the time to seek wisdom and make positive decisions. I valued this advice and applied it, which gave me a firm foundation as my life and career continued to unfold.

Although complicated, the experience with Dr. Rogers taught me that sometimes we find ourselves in circumstances out of our control that are unfortunate or unfair. We can fight our hardest against what we can't control, or we can take charge by choosing a path of resilience. We must first evaluate if fighting will produce desired results or if we need to accept and proceed within the circumstances presented to us. Sometimes surrendering to what we can't change while proactively pushing toward the choices we can impact is the best and wisest option. After much prayer and guidance, I approached the situation with Dr. Rogers in this manner. I accepted the circumstances I was in while affecting the outcome through my attitude.

I didn't know it then, but my choice to make the best of a bad situation would have far-reaching effects. Dr. Rogers grew to respect me and become a mentor to me. He wrote referrals that placed me in jobs and internships. His advice and wisdom were my most significant source of guidance through the first decade and a half of my career. Raising my head high and returning to his class after all that transpired became a marker of resilience that would impact me under far more difficult circumstances.

"I hoped that her beautiful
smile would be something that
I would get to see more often."

4

Meeting Maleka

During the critical timeline block that Dr. Rogers lectured about, one of those life-changing moments occurred in November of 2000 when I met Ms. Maleka Grimes at Tennessee State University in the fall of her senior year. More accurately, I tried to meet her while she had nothing to do with me. Maleka was a resident advisor (RA) for an apartment near my housing unit during that school session. We had orbited around each other for years on campus without ever meeting. Eventually, I had been assigned to live in her apartment building but was switched to a different one before I moved in. I often joke that this was for the best, as it kept her from witnessing any college antics and debauchery that I engaged in while living there. She would not have been amused or impressed by that behavior, and it would have completely ruined any chances of garnering her favor.

Apparently, she wasn't too impressed with me in the first place. Notified that a package for me had been delivered to her building, I went to pick it up, and when I saw how cute she was, I tried to pick her up, too. Even with what I thought were my smoothest moves, she was having none of it.

Maleka was sitting in the reception area of the apartment clubhouse when I approached. I immediately noticed how beautiful she was and tried to capture her attention.

In my best attempt to strike a balance between cool and charming, I said, "Hey, how are you doing?"

Before looking back at the bulky desktop, she briefly glanced up from the computer.

"I'm all right," she replied, unimpressed.

"Great! My name is Ti Jackson, and I had a message on my voicemail that said I had a package here." I leaned casually against the desk.

"Okay, give me a second, and I'll go get it," she replied, her focus never leaving the computer screen.

I tried to engage her attention again. "What are you working on?"

She sighed as if annoyed by the question. "You know Ms. Bass, the apartment complex residence director? She is trying to get me to draw pictures for the complex for some event that she's throwing in the clubhouse this weekend. She gets on my nerves asking me to do these things at the last minute."

"Oh, I'm sorry to hear that. I thought Ms. Bass would be pretty cool. You look really familiar; I know that I've seen you around. What's your name?" I asked, trying to coax some connection.

"Maleka Grimes," she said indifferently.

"Oh, okay. Aren't you an AKA?" I asked, trying to keep the conversation going.

"Yeah."

Her monosyllabic answers weren't helping to advance my cause. Not easily deterred, I persisted. "I know I've seen you around with some of them other AKAs. Who do you hang out with?" I asked.

"You know Ima and Paulisa?" she questioned.

"Yeah, I know them! I know of Ima. I've met Paulisa before. That's who I've seen you with!"

I thought that having some common friends would make her more apt to talk to me. Obviously, I was wrong. She was all business, and I seemed to be getting in her way.

"Oh, okay. What's your apartment number?" she asked, directing the conversation right back to the matter at hand.

"Oh, I live in 2908," I replied.

"Let me go get your package." Maleka left me standing at the desk while she retrieved my delivery. I was used to girls giving me attention, especially when I pulled out the full forces of what my friends called the "Ty-Mac" charm, but she was giving me absolutely no mind.

"Here's your package," she said, handing it to me and immediately returning her focus to her computer screen. There was a brief pause before she exclaimed, "Didn't you used to date one of my line sisters?"

Chagrined, I replied, "Oh, yeah, I did, but that was last year. I don't date any AKAs anymore."

Maleka paused her work for a split second to shoot me a quizzical look. I took her response as my cue to leave.

I continued talking as I made my exit. "I appreciate it," I said with a nod. "Good luck with trying to finish what Ms. Bass wants by this weekend. Thanks again. Don't be a stranger and not speak now when we bump into each other."

"Okay," replied Maleka in a tone that sounded like she meant the opposite of what she had said.

"Maybe we'll run into each other sometime," I called on my way out the door.

Maybe it was my confident nature, or perhaps it was the fact that Maleka had basically ignored me, but after that encounter, I was sure that she was a girl that I wanted to get to know better. Although our meeting was a seemingly insignificant event, it was memorable to me, and I hoped that her beautiful smile would be something that I would get to see more often.

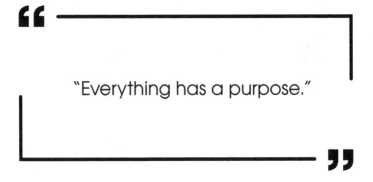

"Everything has a purpose."

5

Pursuing Maleka

February 8, 2001—it was Thursday night at Tennessee State University, and my friends Sam and Reggie talked me into attending a basketball game. Packed with enthusiastic and rambunctious Tiger fans, the Gentry Center was buzzing with excitement for the game. Pumped after receiving a good grade on a test that day, the frenetic vibe of the game suited my celebratory mood. I laughed, talked, and mingled with friends, eventually chatting with a cute girl who gained my attention. She wasn't a student at TSU but was a local who suggested that I meet up with her and her friends at a Nashville club called Outer Limits after the game.

Typically on weeknights, I followed an unusual study habit of working while everyone else was out or sleeping, studying from 11 PM to about 3 AM. After that, I would crash and then rally, waking up in time for a ten or eleven o'clock class. Going to a basketball game wouldn't have put me too far off my schedule, but going to a club on a weeknight definitely would.

The girl was cute, though, and we had struck up a rapport, so I decided to go and meet up with her there.

The music blared in the club as all around me bodies gyrated to the music. Packed with college students, I searched the dim room for any sign of the girl from the basketball game.

Making my way through the jostling of the crowd, I spotted a familiar face sipping on a bright blue drink.

"Hey, TSU! I remember you," I said, gesturing between the two of us.

She looked uninterested.

"What's your name again?" I asked, trying to gain her attention.

"Maleka," she replied dispassionately.

I struck up a conversation with her, and we started chatting. Maleka had graduated from TSU and was working as a middle school teacher. Her friend, Ima, decided they needed a night out, persuading Maleka to join her at the club. We made small talk for a few minutes as I continued to glance around for the girl I was supposed to meet up with. Since she wasn't in sight, I figured that I would ask Maleka to dance.

"Hey, do you want to dance with me?" I prodded.

"No." She shot me down cold. "I just got this drink, and I want to finish it."

I couldn't figure this girl out. She had ignored me on the day we first met, and she definitely didn't want to dance with me now. Her lack of interest bruised my ego, but since I was there to meet another girl anyway, I brushed it off and continued making my way around the club.

The music thumped as I made my way around the room, looking for the elusive girl from the basketball game. She was nowhere to be seen. My search eventually led me face to face with Maleka and her blue drink again.

I eyed the level of her drink. The blue liquid was assuredly lower than before. My eyes captured hers.

"I see that you still have your drink—but it isn't as much. Do you want to dance now?" I queried hopefully.

"No," she said with certainty.

That damn blue drink! I couldn't believe that I had just set myself up to be turned down again. This time, she laughingly assured me that she would dance with me when she was done.

My next search around the club took longer, and I never located the girl who was supposed to meet me. Instead, I found what I had been looking for all along—Maleka. There she was again, and this time, the drink was gone. Somehow I knew that if there was one girl worth pursuing, it was this girl.

I asked her to dance again, bracing myself for the inevitable "No."

"You don't have that drink anymore," I said. "You should dance with me."

"Okay," she said, her eyes twinkling. "I'll dance with you now."

She followed me onto the floor. We danced, talked, laughed, and connected, and by the end of the night, I ended up with her phone number. We didn't have paper, so we wrote our numbers on a gum wrapper that we split in two. We then pocketed each other's number, being sure not to lose it. Our chemistry was magnetic, and we were both drawn to each other in a way that seemed inexplicable.

The funny thing is that in life, where so many things often go wrong, that night was evidence that God used many different things to draw us to that precise moment for a purpose. My friends' cajoling and a good grade on a test led me to go to a basketball game that I would not otherwise have attended. The basketball game led me to a girl who suggested a club I would never have gone to without her influence.

I never saw that girl from the game again. However, I think of her often, because without meeting her, I would never have met Maleka. She brought me to my girl with the blue drink—that damn blue drink! I jokingly swore to Maleka that I would never drink a blue drink because it kept her from connecting with me earlier, and I would not have wanted to waste another second without her.

Everything has a purpose. So many threads were woven together to bring us to each other. The truth is that if months before, I hadn't run into Maleka that day at TSU, where she acted as if I didn't exist, then I would never have recognized her in the club that night and tried to talk to her. That night, so many seemingly random occurrences intertwined in a perfect design to bring me Maleka. I am forever grateful for that.

"Together we were both the

best versions of ourselves."

6

Winning Maleka

After that night at Outer Limit, Maleka and I started to talk regularly. Phone calls led to a first date.

I often prayed, but not typically before I met girls to hang out. However, that night was different. As I pulled into her apartment parking lot, I paused to pray for her and our time together. I didn't know what precisely I was asking the Lord for, but there was just something about Maleka that prompted my plea that night.

> *Dear Lord, I don't know what it is about this girl, but she is special. I don't know your plan for this situation, but I pray that Lord willing, you work this out for good. Please help this date to go well and for me not to say or do anything stupid. Please help me not to mess this up. Amen.*

In college, I had put my faith in a box and packed it away, reveling in the secular nature of being away from home, on a campus, hormones going crazy, and getting caught up with different friends and influences.

I had become undisciplined in my prayer life, only praying when I thought I needed a boost from God— when I wanted help on a test or had gotten myself in trouble. Somehow, though, I knew that Maleka was special, and I prayed for God's favor in that situation.

We ate dinner at Maleka's apartment, where we balanced paper plates of spaghetti on our laps as we picnicked in her living room. She radiated joy and a glow that was so attractive. She seemed so comfortable in her surroundings, which immediately put me at ease. We instantly had chemistry and connection that I had never felt before, and it was as captivating as her personality.

Neither of us were looking to be in a relationship, but Valentine's Day was approaching on the heels of our first meeting. I hadn't anticipated meeting and connecting with Maleka and already had a date scheduled for the holiday with a friend. As the date got closer, I kept thinking that if I were going to do something special for Valentine's Day, I wanted it to be with Maleka. I shared that honestly with my friend, and I felt terrible as I watched the disappointment fall over her face, but I knew it was the right thing to do.

I asked Maleka if she would like to spend Valentine's evening with me. I planned the fanciest dinner that my college budget could buy and treated her to the high-class dining establishment of Red Lobster. Conversation with Maleka combined with delicious crab legs seemed like an ideal date, and we enjoyed ourselves immensely.

As my relationship with Maleka grew, I discovered more and more things that I admired about her. She was beautiful and radiated life—that was obvious to everyone around her. She was well-spoken and intelligent and initially dreamed of taking the LSAT and going to law school. Beyond that, though, were deep aspirations and a drive to succeed while helping others be successful as well. This impressed me, but I was equally impressed by the beauty of her heart and her caring for others.

Maleka was incredibly funny. She could laugh or make a joke out of almost anything. I valued this. I might have a witty one-liner now and then, but it was nothing compared to her silly antics and great sense of humor. The more I was around her, the more I craved being around her.

I had dated other girls before, and none of them measured up to what I found in Maleka. Generally, the more I got to know a girl, the more she wanted out of me as far as taking a piece of my future instead of making her own alongside me. Most girls wanted me to have a good job and make a lot of money, not for my benefit but to benefit them one day. Maleka was never like that. She was well grounded and independent. She wanted to make her own success in life and encouraged me to do the same in my dreams and aspirations. This quality was rare and refreshing in a way that made me want to always be better for her and achieve more. Together we were both the best versions of ourselves.

My birthday fell within a few weeks of our "first official meeting." Maleka made me feel so valued on that day in a way that no one else had done before. She genuinely listened to the things that were important to me and found ways to show me she cared on a tight teacher's budget. I loved chewing on sunflower seeds, and she made sure that I had bags of them for my birthday. I was a big fan of WWE wrestling, The Rock, and "Stone Cold" Steve Austin. Maleka couldn't have cared less about professional wrestling, but she noted that it was important to me, so she bought me a calendar featuring all of my favorite wrestlers. From our Red Lobster date, she knew that I loved crab legs, so she took me out to a restaurant known for its seafood. These were all seemingly simple things, but they meant so much to me. A gifted artist, Maleka poured her time and energy into making me a carefully designed coupon book with redeemable thoughtful gestures from her to me, such as making me dinner or giving me a back rub. I was blown away by the gift of her consideration, her thoughtfulness, and her time. No one had ever showered me with so much kindness, which was significant to me. I had no expectations of anything from her, but she anticipated the needs and desires that I had in a way that was so special and unique to her character and personality. I would gradually discover that this was part of who she was, and I greatly admired that in her.

Maleka was scheduled to walk at her graduation within a few months of our meeting. She had graduated earlier but was part of the end-of-the-year ceremony. Her family and friends came from all over to support her. As she introduced me to her supporters, I realized that things were getting serious, which didn't bother or intimidate me. It felt natural—like all of the pieces were falling into precisely the right place.

"Sometimes you chase dreams, and sometimes you change dreams."

7

Moving Forward

As Maleka and I grew closer, our paths merged, and we began to plan our future together. I was drawn to Maleka's intelligence, her ambition, and her motivation to pursue what was important. We also mutually placed a great value on education. We both wanted to put ourselves in a better future financially and professionally, so we purposely planned for our future success.

Maleka completed her undergraduate degree with the desire of being a teacher while she pursued the longer-term goal of law school. My plan also included advanced degrees as I aspired to complete my undergrad degree in mechanical engineering at TSU, followed by a master's in engineering that I wanted to attain before going into the workforce.

Sometimes you chase dreams, and sometimes you change dreams. Maleka and I changed our goals to include each other as we grew together. There was compromise on both our parts, but that didn't equate to sacrifice. It was essential to both of us that we mutually nurture each other's efforts to excel.

As she started to investigate potential law schools, I realized that I would follow her wherever she wanted to go. I evaluated my options for graduate school and went on several tours and trips, but one thought remained: *I want to be with this woman. I want to go wherever she goes.* That was the priority.

While still at TSU, I was presented with an engineering position with Rolls Royce. I had interned and done co-ops with them, and before I even graduated from college, I had an offer lined up to work there. The dilemma was that if I went to work for Rolls Royce, I would have to delay graduate school. I spoke to several professors and advisors who assured me that following this path would not prevent me from gaining a graduate degree later on.

Maleka obtained a teaching job in Indianapolis, which meant that we could be together, work using the skills acquired in our undergraduate degrees, and position ourselves to obtain higher levels of education. The important thing was that we could continue to grow ourselves while growing together in our relationship.

It wasn't long before we went from dating, to engaged, to married, and to planning for a future family. Maleka had been teaching sixth grade when I met her, but she seemed to take on a younger class grade each year that we lived in Indianapolis. Maleka had a huge heart; it never failed that as she met and grew to know her students, their families, and their home situations, she struggled not to be deeply affected by the weight of what others were carrying. Caring so profoundly was a beautiful gift that made her a fantastic teacher, but it also wore her down as she bore the weight of so many things outside of her control. She often came home crying as her heart broke for her students who were being mistreated at home, were challenged with learning, or had parents who hurt more than they helped. She was doing everything she could to teach them yet felt as if she were never doing enough. I watched her wilt under the weight of other people's burdens, and more than anything, I wanted her to excel.

Eventually, Maleka realized that teaching was weighing too heavily on her, and she could be more effective in a different role. Her mom had been a schoolteacher for over thirty years, and as much as she admired and wanted to emulate that, she was called to go a different path, and I fully supported her in that.

A new job helping people with their trusts and retirements pushed her to realize that she wanted to go back to school to pursue her MBA and move into a new career path. At around the same time, my job at Rolls Royce had identified me as one of thirty employees under the age of thirty who had advanced potential. As such, they honored me with participation that allowed me to get my MBA while working for the company in the hopes that the skills I garnered would benefit the company.

Maleka and I were in different MBA programs at separate universities, but we worked side by side to help push each other toward our goals. We recognized that encouraging each other's dreams and desires made us individually more confident and better-rounded, which poured back into our marriage and strengthened us as a whole.

Maleka became pregnant with our son Cameron as we completed our MBA programs. We hadn't been planning on having any children until we were in our thirties, as we were both driven by career and education. Still, Cameron surprised us and was born three days after Maleka's twenty-seventh birthday. We looked forward to his arrival with eager anticipation and were both determined to raise him in the best possible way. I admired that pregnancy propelled Maleka on in her goals and that she was able to graduate while in her last trimester of pregnancy. She was a wonder to me, and I knew she would be an absolutely incredible mom.

When Cameron was born, Maleka became even more focused. She was adoringly loving and attentive to our sweet son. She expertly juggled caring for him and working from home.

"Cam" looked just like Maleka, but his personality tended to be more similar to mine. It was fascinating to watch him grow and develop his character and interests. If he was into something, he fixated on it. His first main interest was trains, specifically Thomas the Tank Engine. He knew absolutely every fact imaginable about Thomas, his train friends, and trains in general. He thrived on trains for years until he met Minecraft. His interest shifted around the age of eight, and I would arrive home to hear recitations about every possible Minecraft detail and world he was creating. It amused me because I would lose myself in my interests and pursuits in a similar manner, so it was fascinating to see this replicated in Cam.

Cam also interacts with people in a manner that is such an incredible mix of Maleka and me. I love that he reflects pieces of both of us but is also incredibly unique in his own giftings and personality. At first, he is shy and observant, introverted like me. However, once someone meets his comfort level, he will talk and talk, glowing with Maleka's extroverted light.

I coached Cam in sports while Maleka bonded with him over more creative pursuits. They both loved art and would spread out canvases and acrylics on the kitchen table, painting or drawing and talking for hours.

When Cam played sports, I was conscientious about encouraging him, but I also gave him feedback about improving. Maleka would scold me, thinking that I was being too critical. I would poke back at her for going too easy on him. There was a loving push and pull, but we always supported Cameron and each other.

As Cameron grew older, we all settled into a natural rhythm. Maleka would work from home and watch Cam during the day. When I got home from work, we would all have dinner together. Then Cam and I would hang out while Maleka went up to our room for some rest time. After some time together, Cam would make his way to our room, where he would sit and talk with Maleka as he wound down for the evening. They would talk about life, problems, worries, the future, relationships—anything that a mother and son could possibly talk about together. Maleka was Cam's comfort. She was his place of safety, and they understood each other in an extraordinary way.

"Often difficulties in life

prepare us for a more arduous

battle in the future."

8

Not Without Purpose

Often difficulties in life prepare us for a more arduous battle in the future. We usually don't recognize this, complaining about the unfortunate nature or timing of these occurrences without realizing that they strengthen us and make us ready.

At the youthful age of thirty-two, I experienced one of these occurrences. While Maleka and I maintained busy lives, I also did my best to stay fit and active. Typically, I would take Cam with me to the gym and drop him off in the childcare area before I worked out. I was in reasonably good shape. I worked out regularly, played basketball and flag football, and was arrogant enough to believe that I "still had it."

One day, after a heavy leg workout, my legs were absolutely wasted. As I went to change and leave the facility, I noticed some kids in their twenties playing basketball. I thought that I had a few moves left in me, so I joined their game. It was all going well until I went up against a really talented kid who was playing strong defense. Facing off against him, I juked right and went left. As I did, I heard a pop so loud it sounded like a gun had gone off. I had completely blown out my right Achilles. It felt as if someone had hit me in the leg with a baseball bat. The feeling was disorienting. I fell on the hard floor of the gym but tried to pull myself up to walk it off. I collapsed. There's no walking off a blown Achilles tendon.

A reverent hush filled the room as everyone recognized the severity of what had happened and watched the situation unfold. Someone gathered Cam for me from the kids' area as I tried my best to hop my way out of there with my dignity intact.

When I got home, Maleka was concerned as well as annoyed. "Why are you out there trying to play with twenty-year-olds when you are thirty-two?" she lectured.

I put off going to the doctor at first as I hoped my Achilles would somehow magically repair on its own. Obviously, it did not. I could barely put any weight on it, and as a result, I limped around as if something was terribly wrong with me.

I called into work and then didn't move off the couch for four days as I hoped it would recover with enough rest. I don't know what I thought because I had heard and felt it pop. Neither was a good indication that this was a rest-and-ice type of situation.

I tried to return to work, limping around like a bizarre wounded animal, and universally my concerned coworkers advised me to see a physician.

It took me almost a week to go to the doctor. When the doctor examined it, he questioned, "Why have you been trying to walk around on this?"

Maleka was so frustrated with me, and my timing couldn't have been much worse. While she was wrapping up work projects and trying to get everything ready for the Thanksgiving holidays, I was helpless and on crutches. She was working, watching Cam, preparing for Thanksgiving, and now, she was also playing nurse to me. She was aggravated and made sure that I knew that would be the last time I played with guys in their athletic prime.

I had surgery to repair it and was scheduled to do intensive physical therapy. This was my first experience with having to rehabilitate a serious injury. I was motivated to be the strongest that I could possibly be, so I pushed through nearly eight months to get into peak athletic condition. By the time I finished my physical therapy, I was in better shape than when I started. I also recognized that even when the body is damaged, it has an amazing capacity for healing. Mentally this made me sharper as I knew that my body was more capable of recovery than I had ever thought possible.

After rehabbing and repairing, Maleka made sure that I played only with guys my age. She didn't want me to attempt to compete with the young guns and get injured again. Despite this admonition, I would not remain unscathed for long.

Two years later, I played basketball in a non-competitive game for men thirty-five and up. Maleka approved, and I respected her desire to keep me safe. The game wasn't aggressive or intense, but that didn't stop me from going all out. I had an exceptional game, feeling like thirty-five might just be the new twenty-five—except that it wasn't.

The slick pine wood floors, the ball gliding over my fingertips, my skills were on fire as I made a fast break toward the basket. I felt a sharp pop in my left knee as I drove toward the hoop. It gave way, and I collapsed to the floor. I couldn't put any weight on it, so I crawled to the side of the court while the game continued around me. Apparently, the old guys league was more used to body parts giving way during the course of a game. They just dribbled around me as I dragged my way to the sideline. A friend grabbed some ice for me and managed to find a doctor who had been working out nearby. He was most definitely not an orthopedic doctor, but he thought he could help. In denial at the extent of my injury and wanting to avoid surgery, I agreed to let the doctor coach me through some rehab and strengthening. This was an utter failure. I had no strength in my knee at all and was in tremendous pain. I couldn't even push a bike pedal with that leg.

When I finally admitted that I needed to see a physician specializing in orthopedics, I was given the dismaying news. I had torn my ACL, PCL, and patellar tendon. Once again, Maleka was not amused. I spent the Christmas holidays in surgery and lying on the couch while a machine bent and flexed my leg eight hours of the day as part of my surgical recovery.

Maleka and I had plans to attend a Beyoncé and Jay-Z concert two days post-Christmas, but my injury adventures had once again overtaken our holidays. She went with a friend and had a blast, but she was disappointed that I couldn't go with her.

Maleka cared for so many people. In her job, she was always serving and taking care of people. At home, she loved and cared for Cam and me. To help all of the people she supported, she adhered to a strict and very packed schedule. When something threw off her schedule, it wasn't ideal. Although my injuries were accidents, I felt bad that they happened. I didn't want to be helpless and create an additional burden for Maleka. I wanted to pour into her so she could continue what she did best pour into others.

Being injured wasn't good, but it taught me some important lessons. It gave me some perspective about how hard Maleka worked and served our family and others. It reminded me that her influence was important to all of those she affected. I learned that life would throw curveballs, and if we don't adjust and roll with it, we will never be able to move forward.

Most importantly, I learned that I had to heal to be the best version of myself for Maleka and Cam following those injuries. There was a time after the injury or surgery when I was essentially helpless, and during this time, I humbly accepted Maleka's help and was grateful for it. However, I eventually had to stand on my own and to do this, I needed to put in the work with physical therapy to recover fully. I had to earnestly determine to get back to peak performance to fully take care of my family. Sometimes the best thing that we can do for ourselves and others is to heal, and this was a responsibility that I took very seriously.

"We made it a priority to put each other first, and in doing so, it strengthened us both."

9

Transition

Pursue what you love with purpose. Maleka was such a great example of someone who was passionate about the job she did, and that passion manifested in impact. Combining her heart for education with the savvy of her business skills, Maleka began working in higher education. She loved to help others succeed in life and achieve everything that they were capable of and more. Working within the higher education system gave her ample opportunity to do this, and she thrived.

While we lived in Indiana, her position in higher education involved various roles in admissions and career services. She was very focused and reliable, and once she committed to accomplishing something, she would carry it out with excellence.

I continued to work for Rolls Royce and was valued in my position there, being nominated for the Black Engineer of the Year Award. If I stayed with that company, every indication showed that I would have a glowing future.

As Cameron grew, we realized that our location near Indianapolis had suited our career paths, but not our family plans. We wanted Cam to be able to spend time with our family in the South, but that was difficult to do when we lived so far away. Our extended families mainly were spread out between Tennessee and Alabama. Maleka longed for Cameron to grow up surrounded by family and cousins instead of isolated as an only child.

Although both Maleka and I had tremendous career growth and prospects at our companies, Indiana didn't suit Maleka's outgoing personality. She loved being surrounded by people and experiencing new adventures and experiences. Unfortunately, the unpredictability of the winter storms in the Midwest was not compatible with leaving the house on a weekend whim. Every winter, I would watch as Maleka sank into a seasonal depression, sadly staring out the window as it sleeted or rained, dashing her plans again and again.

One year, there were eight straight weekends in which there was snow on the ground, making it impossible to venture out. Maleka sat on our love seat in tears, and it broke my heart.

I knew that this couldn't go on. Maleka always shone with a bright light, and in these long winter months, her light seemed to grow dimmer and dimmer. I hated to witness her struggle, especially if there was something that I could do to improve the situation and alleviate some sadness. It wasn't complicated to see that she needed to be somewhere that nurtured who she was and allowed her to blossom in that vibrancy. My career was important but not at the cost of Maleka's spirit.

We decided to pray about the situation and sincerely devoted ourselves to seeking the Lord on the matter, both separately and together. Then we talked and decided what was best for our family as a whole, with the Lord leading our steps. We decided that we would move somewhere warm and closer to family. As we explored different options and opportunities, we found Atlanta, Georgia, to be a good fit.

As I researched different job possibilities, Maleka helped me to prepare. Interviewing wasn't my strength, but Maleka made a great coach, working with me to practice for success. Due to her experience in career services, she gave me expert guidance as I applied for jobs, and I was so grateful that we made such a strong team.

I interviewed at a company in Atlanta for an engineering role, and once accepted, that secured our decision to move there. Relocating was a bit of a restart for our family. We had to find a new place to live, adjust to a new environment, and alter our career trajectory, but the end result was that we would be surrounded by family support, and that was important.

Within a few months of our arrival in Atlanta, Maleka was hired as the assistant director of career services at a local college and became an immediate asset to their program. Shortly after that, she became a director at Georgia Perimeter College. In that role, she was networking with different companies to find students opportunities for co-ops, internships, and jobs. She connected students with corporations. Eventually, she became drawn to the corporate side of things and wanted to transition into the opposite role of what she had been doing. Instead of advocating for the students from the educational side, she found that she could transition to the corporate side and have a more significant impact, creating new opportunities for students that might not have otherwise existed. This excited her, and she went back to school to pursue another graduate degree, this time in human resources.

This experience led her to carve out a niche role for herself, allowing her to identify students for diversity and inclusion roles and executive positions at various corporations. Each position she held, job title that she had earned, and higher education degree she attained became stair steps for her to reach this vital role that she loved. It combined her passion for students with a desire to open doors for minorities within the corporate world, and she thrived on this.

As Maleka obtained a second master's degree, I also had the opportunity to attain an additional master's degree from Georgia Tech in systems engineering. Once again, we found ourselves able to excel in our career and educational aspirations, encouraging each other and setting a good example for Cameron.

Propelling Maleka toward excellence didn't set me back in my career. If she moved forward in her success, she pulled me ahead in my purpose. If I thrived in my career, it would help to slingshot her forward as well. We made it a priority to put each other first, and in doing so, it strengthened us both.

This also made us better parents for Cameron, as pursuing our gifts gave us great joy that we then transferred into him. As Cameron grew, we continued to connect with him in our own unique ways. I would play video games with him and coach him in sports. Maleka continued to nurture his creative pursuits and his playful side. Often I would come home to find music blasting as they both danced throughout the house, smiles blazing across their cheeks and laughter overflowing.

Cameron's love for Maleka was evident. Aside from his beloved Boston terrier, Indiana Jones, Maleka was Cameron's closest confidant and refuge for conversation. Just as she inspired everyone she worked with, she motivated our family to draw closer and cherish our bond.

We worked extremely hard during the year, but we also made time for fun and relaxation. Family vacations were important, but Maleka and I also prioritized special trips as a couple. Cam never seemed to mind, as he would go on his own adventures to stay with and be spoiled by his favorite family members during that time. Vacations allowed Maleka and me to spend special time together reconnecting, and we did so with intention.

"It is strange how sometimes
a simple act such as going
one direction or another
or choosing one seat over
another can change
your life forever."

10

The Bahamas

July 27, 2018—I struggled to focus on work in the days leading up to our vacation. I worked Monday and Tuesday, but my brain was already dreaming of my trip to the Bahamas with Maleka. She had been away on a business trip to Chicago, working hard in an interim position to lead to a promotion. We both looked forward to having a break and vacation, celebrating our fifteenth wedding anniversary.

I drove Cameron up to Nashville to stay with Maleka's brother Shan and sister-in-law in preparation for our getaway. They lived only about fifteen minutes away from my sister, ReVonda. The plan was to drop off Cameron and stop in for a visit with ReVonda and her husband, Greg, but I was running behind and had to substitute the visit with a phone call. ReVonda had been to the Bahamas before, and we had a long conversation as she gave me all sorts of tips and recommendations for our stay.

I was simply ReVonda's annoying little brother when we were growing up. She was responsible for watching me, playing with me, and babysitting me. If she brought boys to the house, I would rope them in as my playmates for Monopoly, chess, video games, etc. Her husband, Greg, was the one guy I didn't manage to scare off. She married him when I was eleven years old. Since ReVonda was ten years older than I was, we didn't have a super close emotional connection in our childhood. She took on more of a protector or overseer role.

Our relationship evolved into a close friendship during my years at TSU. She and Greg lived in Nashville, so we started to spend more time together. Soon enough, ReVonda became my sounding board for wisdom and advice. She relished meeting my friends and giving me wisdom on dating, relationships, women, and marriage. She loved Maleka dearly and helped me to cherish my marital relationship.

Leading up to the Bahamas trip, my sister and I usually talked about once a week; we joked about funny things our mom did, caught up, and shared our lives. This conversation was no different—we bantered and laughed, and I informed her of our plans for the trip. She was excited for Maleka and me to get away from some relaxation and wished us the best as our phone call ended.

The next day, Maleka and I prepared to leave on an early flight. Maleka valued time. She was always extremely busy and therefore measured in her approach to scheduling. She liked to be early. I favored the later side of on-time. It was interesting to see our approaches to punctuality duel whenever we traveled. I had the habit of pushing us a little closer to time than Maleka would have liked, but that morning we made it to the airport and through security with an abundance of time.

We had a drink together at the bar—not a blue drink, though; we still stayed away from those. We were in a celebratory mode, toasting to Maleka's promotion and our anniversary. We were determined to have a memorable vacation.

Our plane landed in Georgetown in the Bahamas, and a bus arrived to shuttle us to the private Sandals Emerald Bay Resort on the shores of Exuma. We hadn't made many plans for our trip as the resort was all-inclusive. There was only one item on Makela's bucket list for the trip. She desperately wanted to see the legendary swimming pigs from the island, so we made plans to do that later in our visit.

When we arrived at the resort, we were in awe. The white sand views of the turquoise waves were breathtaking, and the weather was perfect. We toured the resort and had a decadent meal together while waiting for our rooms to be ready. We eventually made our way poolside. The extravagant pools with a swim-up bar made for a great spot to launch our holiday in paradise.

Maleka glowed in the shimmering sun. She couldn't swim but relaxed on a float in the pool as she began to talk with other vacationers. She was gifted at making instant connections, and these circumstances were no different. Everyone loved Maleka, and her vibrant personality and cheerful nature drew people in, making instant friendship connections. She was magnetic. More introverted in personality, I admired this skill, and it challenged me to better connect with others.

We talked with other couples who gave us tips about what to do and see during our stay. It was nice to have time together to relax and socialize with other couples. We felt reinvigorated by this special time together.

On Friday evening, Maleka and I had a private photo shoot on the beach to commemorate our anniversary and our time together. This was followed by dinner and a visit to the resort's piano bar. A round of karaoke started, and Maleka was quick to join in. She loved to sing and be surrounded by people, so she was fully in her element. I loved watching my wife enjoy life to the fullest.

The next day, Saturday, June 30th, Maleka and I woke up, had breakfast together, and made our way to the shuttle that would take us to our tour. Given Maleka's propensity for promptness, we arrived at the resort bus stop fifteen minutes before our scheduled shuttle. We were the first couple there. When we finally were situated on the bus, we began chatting with an engaging couple named Chris and Stacy Clark, whom we connected with immediately. They were from Houston, where Chris was an offensive lineman in the NFL. As you might expect, Chris was a big guy, given his vocation. At 6'5" and over 300 pounds, he towered over my 5'9" frame. Maleka and I established an instant rapport with the Clarks; they were kind and easy to talk to. We were a little disappointed to learn that we would be going on separate tours. They were doing the full-day tour option, and we had registered for the half-day choice.

When we got to the marina, we were funneled into a slow-moving line toward the registration and our boat tours. Couples chatted around us excitedly in anticipation of the adventure.

I wasn't necessarily excited to go on this particular excursion, but Maleka was, and that was what mattered. I had a round of golf scheduled for the next day, so we were both getting a chance to relax by doing something of interest to us, and that was important.

Once through the line, we were directed to walk down the dock where boats waited to take us on our tours. Our boat for the half-day excursion was on the left and the boat for the full-day excursion was on the right.

It is strange how sometimes a simple act such as going one direction or another or choosing one seat over another can change your life forever. We often think that minor decisions don't matter in the grand scheme of life without realizing that sometimes the smallest choice can impact your life forever.

Maleka and I were the first people on the boat, so we got to choose whatever seats seemed appealing to us. We made our way to the middle of the boat and chose the third row back on the right. I sat next to the aisle, and Maleka had a seat next to the side. There were snacks and drinks provided on the boat, so we settled in and prepared for a fun trip. The catamaran gradually filled with other people as the captain and his twelve-year-old "mate" readied for launch. The boat was only half capacity, with ten passengers eagerly anticipating the tour.

I had my phone out earlier to take pictures but had been instructed by the touring company to put it away until we left the dock, so I carried my phone and Maleka's in my backpack. She insisted that I check to make sure that it would be ready for pictures, and I assured her that I would take it back out at the proper time. Maleka and I chatted about the beautiful day as we glanced at the glistening cerulean swirls in the pale aquamarine water around us. The captain started talking, following a script to engage us and draw forth laughter. My swim trunks rustled as I crossed my left foot over my right knee to better position myself for the view. I draped an arm around Maleka, leaning in closer to this woman that I loved so much.

As the boat pulled out of the marina, I surveyed the white sandy shores dotted with copses of blossoming trees and arrayed in all the splendor of God's creation. The boat rhythmically rocked as it glided over small waves toward open water. As I pulled Maleka closer, I watched her radiant smile illuminated by the sunlight and the joy radiating from her. Everything in that moment seemed so perfect, a pristine portrait of the beauty of life.

In an instant, everything changed.

Part II

The Accident

"Instinctively, I knew that I had to move or I would die in the inferno surrounding me."

11

Explosion

A few minutes into our boat ride, a sound like a shotgun blast reverberated through the air, the fuel tank directly underneath our seats exploding as the force of the explosion lifted the starboard pontoon completely clear of the water before it crashed back into the waves below. I heard none of this.

The entire right side of the boat went up in flames. Maleka and another passenger were hurled from the craft into the water below, debris from the discharge littering the waves. Thrown onto the bottom of the boat, my face landed within inches of a metal pole affixed to the floor. In retrospect, I recognize that I had narrowly missed a severe head injury or impalement had I landed even two inches closer to that railing.

I lay where I landed in a rapidly growing crimson river of my own blood. Flames gyrated around me as smoke filled the air. Injured passengers scurried to get off the boat's wreckage while I lay unconscious. One man tried to assist me, shrieking at me to wake up while trying to drag my lifeless body toward safety.

When his efforts proved futile, he rushed to save himself, abandoning me and swimming toward the other boat.

I came to face down on the floor of the boat. Smoke filled my nostrils, the air scented with the putrid smell of burning meat. Disoriented, I struggled to figure out where I was and what had occurred.

What is happening? I thought, my mind trying to make sense of what was going on around me.

I lifted my head, slightly shifting my body in an attempt to assess the situation. Then I saw it. One of my legs was twisted in a hauntingly bizarre angle, bone visibly protruding from a profusely bleeding open wound. It looked as if my left leg was no longer attached to my body.

Horror overtook me as I realized that the burning smell of meat wasn't a friendly summertime barbecue but was the roasting of my extremity. One leg was utterly mangled or gone, and the other leg was on fire. I smelled the burning of my flesh before my mind signaled the accompanying searing pain. *I was on fire!* Panic began to well inside me.

Maleka! My eyes searched frantically to try to locate her. I tried to calm myself as I scanned the boat looking for anyone that could help. I saw no one.

The flames were growing in intensity, the heat radiating off them in unrelenting waves as the thick black smoke billowed through the air, staining the sky an obsidian hue. I raised my head again, relieved when my eyes landed on the second tour boat floating just a few hundred feet in the distance.

"Get off the boat!" I heard the frantic screams of passengers from the other vessel futilely trying to signal me to safety.

I tried to push myself up, but my arms collapsed. *Get off the boat!* Flames licked at my body as I tried to continue forward, my arms failing and my legs useless to help. Instinctively, I knew that I had to move or I would die in the inferno surrounding me. My left arm was severely impaired, but my right arm seemed to be working. I stretched it forward, grasping onto anything that it could reach. My fingertips made contact with the tiny grooves on the floor of the boat. I pawed at the metal ridges, desperately searching for traction. Dragging myself by my fingertips, I pulled inch by inch in an agonizing haul toward the edge of the boat.

I need to get the hell away from this boat!

A guttural cry of pain tore from my lips as my fingertips scratched and scraped at the floor of the boat, trying to gain traction against the ground as I continued my slow crawl toward the open ledge of the aluminum catamaran.

The effort was excruciating, but I persisted, slowly propelling myself forward with each grasp and grab of my fingertips. The edge of the boat in sight and just a few short drags away, I passed out, the flames seeking to engulf me.

Movement around me signaled panic as the cries of passengers from the other tour boat scrambled and screamed, afraid for their safety. Some of them yelled to move their boat away from ours, terrified that their vessel would meet the same fate.

A few heroic individuals dove into the water, swimming toward danger, determined to find a way to get me and others off of the burning boat. Facing the flames, they climbed aboard, strong arms hoisting me into the waiting hands of others in the water below.

Carrying me as if cradling a small child, the towering NFL football player that we had met on the bus, Chris Clark, waded through the water with me in his arms, my left leg dangling in a painful disconnect as bacteria and water poured in through the open wounds. My body was no longer on fire, yet the burning was agonizing.

"Where's Maleka? Where's my wife? Where's Maleka?" I rasped before passing out again from the intensity of the pain.

"You are strong. You are going

to survive. Keep fighting."

12

You Are a Fighter

As the skeletal shell of the boat blazed in the water, the other injured passengers and I were placed on a small fishing craft to return to shore. I floated in and out of consciousness as worry for Maleka competed with the torrents of relentless pain assaulting my body.

Local workers and passengers gathered sheets of plywood and wooden beams, producing makeshift stretchers to carry the broken bodies of the severely injured to nearby vehicles for transportation to a nearby medical clinic. Chris helped load my plywood pallet into the back of the truck and then climbed in with me, his massive frame hunching over the wreckage of my body as I lay moaning in the bed of the pickup truck.

"Where's Maleka? Where's my wife?" I groaned out those words on repeat.

The truck pulled away from the dock, each bump and shift an agonizing onslaught of sickening pain. Delirious and concerned for my wife's safety, I tried to soothe myself by controlling what I could do instead of focusing on the pain ripping through my body as the pickup careened down bumpy back roads, each jolt and shift an agonizing assault. Chris tried to keep me conscious, reassuring me and focusing my mind on what needed to be done instead of what I was enduring.

I have always found refuge and calm in numbers, and in these circumstances, it was no different. I needed to organize my thinking, and Chris helped me. I told him that my mom would need to be called and informed of what happened. I repeated her phone number over and over again, hoping that he would remember. My sister's number came next, and then my hotel room number and combination for the safe. Somehow I had the presence of mind to realize that someone might need to retrieve our passports from the stash inside our room at the resort. I repeated the numbers several times, hoping that Chris would remember them and reach out to my family. Chris dutifully memorized each number, an impressive feat given the stress and intensity of the circumstances that we were in. He stayed by my side the entire journey to the clinic. His wife accompanied Maleka in another truck as we sped toward help.

Physically, the truck ride was brutal, and the pain was more excruciating than anything that I had ever experienced in my life. My foot lay dangling in the truck bed and my body roared with torment as we navigated rock-filled and unfinished roads toward medical care. After ten or fifteen minutes on the road, the truck stopped to pick up a passenger. A young EMT, who seemed to be just a boy, climbed into the truck to try to assist. He tried to speak with me, but his accent was so thick that I could barely understand him at all.

"Where's my wife? Where's my wife?" I asked him repeatedly.

"She's going to the clinic," was all he said that I could understand. Scared for her safety, I was relieved to know that she was already on her way to get care.

I began to pray, *God, you know the circumstances. Why did this happen? Please be with my wife. Please protect Maleka. Please help us to be okay.* I pleaded over and over with the Lord as I faded in and out of consciousness.

As the truck pulled up to the clinic, my wooden pallet was replaced with a stretcher, and I was carried into a trauma bay. Flat on my back, I couldn't survey the scene around me, but I heard the sounds of crying and moaning. *Maleka!*

Thin curtains separated three patient bays about ten feet wide. Maleka was in the first bay, a young woman named Stefanie Shaffer was in the second, and I was positioned in the third. Other passengers had been injured in the explosion, but our injuries were the most extensive, and our care was given priority.

Maleka! God, please keep my wife safe.

Alone in my bay, I tried to calm my racing heart, taking deep breaths and finding relief in the fact that Maleka was being tended to. I could hear staff working on her, and I prayed that she was getting the care she needed. My injuries could wait if that meant that my wife was getting the medical attention that she needed.

The yelling continued, and I realized it came from the bay next to me. Stefanie Schaffer cried out in agony as she bravely fought for her life. Her cries intermingled with Maleka's as I deliriously uttered silent prayers for help.

Please be okay, Maleka!

Searing spasms of pain ripped through my body, but I tried to stay calm despite the torment. My mind tried to make sense of what was going on, and I tried to rationalize things, hoping that Maleka would make it.

Chris had been with me the entire truck ride, and he had repeatedly told me, "It will be okay." I figured that since he had witnessed the whole thing and had seen Maleka's condition, she must not be as bad as I thought. We just had to get through this, and she would be all right. She would be all right.

I clung to that as I heard the distress of her cries emanating from the other bay. I was in shock. I couldn't move. My leg was awkwardly positioned on the stretcher, my ankle bone protruding as my foot dangled from it, a steady seeping of blood puddling around it.

The EMT that had climbed into the truck with me would check on me every ten minutes or so just to be sure that I was still alive, but otherwise, I was all alone. The sounds of the shrieking women tore at my soul as I listened to try to gather any information that I could, sifting through the shouts and screams to try to grasp any sounds or conversations that would reassure me that Maleka was going to be all right. I didn't fully realize the significance of the trauma that my own body had been through, as I ached for positive news about my wife.

The clinic was a bare-bones operation. It wasn't equipped for high-level traumas. It was a place for treating basic ailments and illnesses, but nothing significant. A handful of nurses attended to patients, and upon news of the boating accident, a doctor was called in, arriving to treat us.

After lying alone for a long time, I was given pain medicine to numb the pain, and someone attempted to address my leg. Instead of cleaning it and attending to it as needed, someone applied medical tape to try to hold it back together. The rest of my injuries were ignored while the medical staff attended to Maleka and Stefanie.

Every once in a while, a staff member would check in on me in my bay before hurrying out toward the moans of Maleka and Stefanie. Every time they left me, I would find comfort in knowing that they were taking care of my wife.

That's okay. I would rather you be with her. Please take care of my precious Maleka.

The EMT from the pickup truck came back into my bay and stayed with me for a while. He tried to ask me general questions, but I struggled to understand what he was saying, his thick accent making the words difficult to understand. My mind was already in a fog; I fought to decipher his words, often guessing their meaning.

"Where's my wife. How's my wife?" I asked on repeat, hoping for news.

My pain-addled brain tried to search through the sounds of his heavy Bahamian accent to grasp at some small glimmer of hope. He replied without emotion, and I thought that I made out the words, "Oh, she's good. Oh, she's good."

There was so much chaos in the clinic as the doctor and nurses bustled about that when Maleka's screams finally faded into silence, I found respite in the hope that she had been tended to and was relieved of pain. I also found reassurance in the words of the EMT.

Maybe Maleka and I would both get through this, and everything would be okay.

Pulling back the curtain to my bay, the doctor entered the room. "You need to go to the hospital in Nassau. We can't do anything here, and you need medical attention. You need to go there so that they can treat you. There is an airplane coming to pick you up."

"What about my wife? What about Maleka?" I asked as the doctor indicated that it would just be Stefanie and me on the flight. "Why isn't Maleka going on this flight?"

The doctor avoided answering me, but I was undeterred. I couldn't understand why they wouldn't be sending Maleka on the same flight or even before me unless her condition was less severe than mine. I tried to make sense of it as I continued questioning the physician.

"She will come later," he replied.

"What does that mean? Will she be on another flight? Is there a second plane waiting to transport her, or is the plane going to fly us there and then come back and pick her up?" I wanted to see my wife and make sure that she would make it out of this ordeal.

He paused before replying, "We are working on getting her there, too."

This news brought me comfort as I figured that Maleka must not be in the same dire condition as Stefanie and me, or they would prioritize her trip on the air ambulance first. I imagined that since her screams and cries had subsided, she must be stable and more comfortable. This thought brought me a measure of peace as they prepared me for an ambulance ride to the transport that would fly us to Nassau.

While I waited, I prayed quietly to myself, *Lord, please help everything to be okay. Please be with Maleka. Please help us to both make it out of this situation.* Over and over, I prayed, asking the Lord to intercede for us both.

As I prayed, from the corner of my eye, I caught a glimpse of Stefanie's stretcher; she was moaning and crying, screaming out in pain as they prepared her for the flight.

God, please help everything to be all right.

Stefanie and I were loaded into an ambulance. Stefanie's mother was allowed to accompany us, speaking words of encouragement to us both as we sped toward the waiting air transport.

She told me, "You are a fighter. I saw you on the boat and witnessed how hard you fought to get yourself to safety. You are strong. You are going to survive. Keep fighting."

It didn't cross my mind to ask her about Maleka. I felt confident that she was medically stable. Stefanie's mother encouraged me, giving me strength and fortitude with her words.

I told her, "You know, my wife is going to be okay."

She didn't reply to my statement about Maleka, except to reassure me that I would make it and that Stefanie and I would both pull through.

Stefanie's mom gave me inspiration and hope, and I clung to the belief that Maleka must be doing better than Stefanie and me. I just needed to survive for her. I tried to stay calm and not let panic pull me under.

The air transport to the hospital was terrifying. Stuck flat on my back with very little room between my face and the structure above me, I felt claustrophobic and fearful. I tried to slow my breathing and prayed to keep myself calm.

Fading in and out of consciousness, I prayed, *Lord, Please help me survive this. Please be with Maleka.*

"My sister was given the horrible news that there had been a boating accident in the Bahamas, and Maleka and I had been in it."

13

There's Been an Accident

Chris Clark began working behind the scenes while I was en route to the hospital in the air transport. When we first burst through the doors of the clinic, Chris was separated from me for the first time since carrying my broken body out of the water. Completely invested in my survival, he tried to gain access and information, insisting to the clinic staff that I was his cousin and he needed to be informed of what was going on. Relentless in his attempt to get updates and ensure that Maleka and I were being cared for, he persisted in doing what he could to ensure our well-being.

Although they had met us only three hours prior, Chris took his promise to contact my mom and my sister seriously and placed the calls as soon as he had shareable information. At that point, after overhearing the doctor give an update on Maleka's status, they were more aware of the situation than I was. Before representatives from the resort arrived and ushered Chris and Stacy away from the clinic and back to their hotel, they were already making calls.

As I was flown to the other hospital, the Clarks started working the phones. Chris, a man of his word, reached out to my mother to let her know what had occurred.

My sister, ReVonda, was enjoying an afternoon at the nail salon when a call came in from our mother. Typically, our mom expects us to reach out to her, not vice versa, so this call immediately put ReVonda on alert.

"Momma, what's going on?" she said into the phone.

My mom calmly replied, "There's a guy on my home phone, and he keeps telling me that Ti has been in an accident."

"An accident?" ReVonda repeated, her panic rising.

"Yeah," replied my mom.

"I think that someone is pranking me. They called and said that Ti and Maleka were in a boating accident." Baffled, my mom thought someone might be playing a sick joke on her.

"Wait a minute, Momma." ReVonda knew that Maleka and I were in the Bahamas and was instantly concerned. "Where did he say the accident was?"

"I don't know," said my mom. "He keeps getting cut off. He said that he was calling from somewhere else."

"Momma, give whoever you are talking to my number and tell them to hang up with you and call me," my sister asserted.

"Oh, okay, well, hold on just a second," Mom huffed.

Chris and Stacy called my sister together, explaining the situation gently. As she sat in her car outside of the nail salon, my sister was given the horrible news that there had been a boating accident in the Bahamas, and Maleka and I had been in it. Chris was hesitant to share much, but ReVonda pushed for more information.

"I don't think your sister-in-law ... I don't think Maleka made it." His voice broke and trailed off.

ReVonda was stunned into silence. She struggled to regain her composure enough to ask for needed information. "Are you sure?" she pressed, a flood of fear engulfing her. "What about my brother?"

"I don't know," he replied. "He's been transported. I don't know."

The call dropped as ReVonda sat there stunned.

"My mind couldn't grasp the words swimming past me as they swallowed me in a sea of overwhelming sorrow."

14

Where's Maleka?

The thirty-minute flight to Nassau was a blur as the pain medication pulled me under into a state of restless unconsciousness. When the air transport landed at the hospital in Nassau, I was met with a buzz of doctors and nurses attending to my care. The clinic had been less than a scant operation, but this hospital had energy similar to what I would expect from a typical emergency room. A group of doctors and nurses started working on me right away, trying to assess the full extent of my injuries.

The medical staff cut my clothes from my body to properly evaluate and determine a plan of action. They took my vitals, administered pain medication, and inserted an IV. A black doctor with a bald head and commanding presence told me they would have to take me to surgery. He said they would give me an MRI and CAT scan, administer anesthesia, and then operate. Barely coherent from all the pain medication now roaring through my veins, I kept asking, "Where's my wife? Where's Maleka? Did her plane make it here yet?"

Their only answer was that I needed to be calm as they prepared me for surgery. Concern for Maleka overshadowed any calm that I had as I desperately wanted to see her, hear her voice, or anything to reassure me that she was not suffering as I was.

I was given no such reassurance as they wheeled me into the operating room to attempt to reattach my foot. Part of my ankle bone had been completely blown from my leg in the explosion, so they tried to piece it back together using various screws and other hardware in place of where bones had been.

When I awoke from surgery, I was in a hospital bed, my left leg wrapped in an enormous bandage. Machines beeped around me as my vitals were monitored and pain medication dripped intravenously into my arm.

A hospital administrator was there with a handful of doctors. I was still groggy, but my focus remained on Maleka. I asked the administrator, "Where's my wife? Is Maleka here? Where is she?"

She quickly hustled everyone out of the room. After a few moments, she returned alone.

"I am sorry, sir," she said gently. "We didn't know if you knew or not, but your wife passed away. She died before you left the clinic. We didn't want to tell you before you went into surgery."

The pain of loss tore through me worse than any agony I experienced in the explosion. Maleka was my life—my wife, my best friend, the mother to our child. *Why? No, not Maleka. God, take me instead. Not Maleka!*

"Your collarbone is broken in four places ... fractured leg ... burns throughout your body ... we couldn't locate some bones in your ankle ... infection ... blood loss..." The administrator kept talking, calmly informing me of the situation.

Why was she still talking when none of that even mattered? My mind couldn't grasp the words swimming past me as they swallowed me in a sea of overwhelming sorrow. My broken body didn't even compare to the heartbreak of losing Maleka.

Left alone in my room, I sobbed uncontrollably. Shattered, the anguish of grief was excruciating.

Why God? Why her? Why not me? Why take Maleka instead of me? How is this fair? Why would you do this? She didn't deserve this.

Hurt, heartbroken, sad, and scared, I questioned God, pleading with Him for some answers or something to be different.

I replayed everything that had occurred in my mind, trying to bring about a different outcome. *Was Maleka really gone? Maybe they made a horrible mistake, and someone else's loved one had been lost. Hadn't the EMT said, "Oh, she's good. Oh, she's good," when I asked how Maleka was doing? Did he lie to me, too?*

In a sickening realization, it dawned on me that I had misinterpreted what the EMT actually said. I had been so desperate for a ray of reassurance that I had projected the best. His words masked in his Bahamian accent had been, "Oh, she's dead. Oh, she's dead."

Helpless physically, all I could do was lie in the bed, overcome by the hauntingly heartbreaking emotions of loss.

"She didn't know if I was alive
or dead but prayed that I
was still holding on."

15

Help Is on the Way

ReVonda sat in her car, impatient to get more details. Turning over and over in her mind the information she had received, she dialed Chris's number.

When Chris was finally able to reconnect, he put his wife Stacy on the phone with my sister, and she tried to answer the barrage of questions coming from ReVonda.

"Stacy, are you sure? Are you sure this is my sister and my brother?" ReVonda questioned in disbelief. "Are you sure?"

She asked her repeatedly to confirm while pressing for answers about both of us. Both Chris and Stacy felt uncomfortable sharing more than they thought they should, but finally, Stacy confirmed the worst.

ReVonda asked, "Is Maleka really gone? Are you positive?"

Somberly, Stacy confirmed, "She's gone. I am positive. We are standing here in the clinic, and she is covered with a sheet. She's not here with us anymore."

ReVonda's complete concern then turned to me. "Where's my brother? Stacy, can you do me a favor? Can you lay eyes on my brother?"

Stacy replied that she couldn't because I had been transported.

"So, he was still alive when he left?" ReVonda questioned, searching for even the smallest gleam of hope.

Before hanging up the call with my sister, Stacy confirmed that I had been alive when I left but was in bad shape.

Overwhelmed with grief and the knowledge that she had to do something, ReVonda put her emotions aside to sift through ideas and options of what she could do to help save my life. She detached from what she couldn't control to maintain a laser-like focus on the things that she could impact.

My sister was in Nashville, and my mom was in Alabama. So, the first thing that ReVonda did was to figure out a way to get my mom up to Nashville so they could travel together to the Bahamas. My mom had called various members of our family to inform them of the accident and to rally support. As soon as she heard what happened, my aunt volunteered my Uncle Andrew to retrieve my mom. My mom's youngest brother, Andrew, made arrangements to pick her up and drive her to ReVonda.

"How long do I pack for?" my mom asked ReVonda.

"It doesn't matter," replied ReVonda. "Just throw some clothes in a bag and bring your passport. We can buy anything that we forget to bring."

ReVonda and her husband, Greg, immediately began working the phones and social media to try to contact Maleka's family so they could be lovingly informed that there had been an accident. They didn't feel that it was their place to tell them anything beyond that, as aside from the phone call with Chris and Stacy Clark, they had no real confirmation themselves. They also tried to contact the United States Embassy in the Bahamas but were initially unsuccessful, as the embassy told them they couldn't release any information at that time.

ReVonda kept a constant stream of calls flowing to the embassy. By Saturday evening, she had gathered enough information to realize that I would most likely be receiving treatment at one of two major hospitals on the island—one was a private hospital, and the other was public. Her Bahamian contacts told her that the private hospital was the more likely of the two, as that is usually where Americans were treated. Armed with this knowledge, she began a barrage of calls to the hospital.

At first, no one would give her any information. They would not confirm that I was there or answer any of her questions. Undeterred, she kept calling, demanding that someone at least answer whether I was at that hospital or not. Eventually, her persistence paid off, and she was directed to a doctor who confirmed that I was indeed at that hospital. She asked him question after question, and he would give her no further information. All she had to go on was that I was hospitalized in the private hospital at Nassau. She didn't know if I was alive or dead but prayed that I was still holding on.

"If I couldn't fight for my life,

she would fight for me."

16

Not Forgotten

That night at the hospital, the nurses attempted to keep my strength up by feeding me a gruel composed of cornmeal and water. This seemingly simple act was too much for me to process. It highlighted my helpless state, emphasizing everything that I had lost. My wife was gone, and my body was so broken that I couldn't even move to feed myself.

I cried and cried and cried all night, sobbing myself in and out of bouts of IV drug-induced sleep, praying that when I woke up, I would realize that it had all been just a horrible nightmare—a bad dream that would disappear by morning.

Unfortunately, this was not to be the case. I woke up around three or four in the morning to the hum of the machines. Unable to lift myself or sit up, my eyes searched around the room until they landed on the blinking lights of the vitals machines. I could see my blood pressure stats, and I knew that at 150/100, my blood pressure was much higher than my usual 135/85. Something didn't feel right.

Soon, medical staff began administering medication to try to lower the pressure. Pain meds were pushed as they tried their best to keep me stable and comfortable, but this was an impossible task. I was in a tremendous amount of physical discomfort, completely forlorn and dependent on others for care, and distraught over the loss of Maleka.

Other than the fact that there was an explosion on the boat and that Maleka was gone, I didn't know anything else that had transpired. I didn't know what had caused the accident or any details surrounding it. I drifted in and out of a grief-saturated state of sleep as the hours continued to drag by.

By 9:15 AM the following day, a United States Embassy representative named Jason was at my bedside. He began issuing a series of questions that felt intrusive, but I also knew they were necessary. Not in a state of mind to be quizzed, I reluctantly participated as he began to ask me for information.

"What are the names of your wife's parents? What is the best way to contact them?" He asked question after question. I also gave him my mom and sister's names and numbers so that he could reach them and inform them of what had happened. He called, but at first he reached no one. I kept giving him various numbers to try, and eventually, he contacted my manager from work. Given the amount of medication I was on, I am not sure that I made much sense, but I struggled through tears to relay to him what happened.

Jason and I kept attempting to contact family and arranged notifications, but we had no idea of everything that had transpired behind the scenes from the moment of the accident or that Chris Clark had honored his word to me and had made the difficult phone calls as promised.

As Jason met with me, ReVonda was already on the move. As soon as she confirmed where I was hospitalized, she immediately asked her husband Greg to book flights. Her little brother was in trouble, and if he was injured as badly as it seemed, he needed people in his corner to fight for him. I couldn't have asked for a better advocate.

Greg booked the flights for ReVonda, and my mother and sister requested that he go, too. She assembled a team to fight for me and knew that Greg would be her greatest helpmate and support, assisting her as he had done throughout their marriage.

Unsure of when they would be returning, ReVonda, Greg, and my mom purchased one-way tickets into Nassau to leave within less than twenty-four hours of their notification about the accident. When they arrived at the airport, they were told that they could not travel one-way on international tickets and had to choose a date to return. Uncertain of the circumstances they would find me in, they did their best to plan with the sparse knowledge that they had.

As they were making arrangements, news of the accident made its way around my social circles. Rushed into surgery once I arrived in Nassau, I was unaware that anyone outside of the Bahamas knew about the accident.

One of my best friends from college, Chris Jones, heard about the accident and pitched in to help. My son Cameron's godfather, I had known Chris since I was nineteen years old. We had gone to school together and worked together, and I considered him part of my family. Hearing about the accident and the arrangements being made by ReVonda to go to the Bahamas, Chris sprang into action. Resourceful, by the time that my family had landed from their first flight to board their connecting flight, Chris had gotten the phone numbers of my mom, Greg, and ReVonda, texting them that there would be a car waiting for them when they landed at the airport in the Bahamas.

As Chris was texting them about the car, ReVonda received a call from the embassy. The representative told her that he was there at the hospital with me.

"You're at the hospital with Ti?" she quizzed.

"Yes. I am standing in his room talking to him," Jason confirmed.

"You tell my brother that we will be there in two hours," she instructed.

"Two hours?" he asked in disbelief.

She explained that they had already found out about the accident and were about to board a connecting flight in Florida that would be in the Bahamas within ninety minutes. ReVonda said that they would be driving from there straight to the hospital.

"You tell my brother that we will be with him in two hours," she repeated, emphatic that I receive the message.

Arriving at the airport in the Bahamas, they found Chris Jones to be true to his word. A driver was there holding a sign with their last name, "Hawkins," and waiting to drive them wherever they needed to go. The driver introduced himself as "Uncle Lou" and immediately took my family under his wing. News travels fast on the island, and somehow, without being told, he knew exactly what hospital they needed to go to locate me. The knowledge that they were being taken care of and directed, even in a place unknown to them, encouraged them and relieved some of their burdens.

ReVonda, my mom, and Greg had entered the hospital through the emergency area, shocked to encounter conditions worse than they could have imagined. A sickening mixture of blood and urine stained the facility as patients lay on the hard floor of the hallways with not enough beds to hold them. Made worse by the one-hundred-degree heat, the smell of festering infection overwhelmed as the cries and moans of patients stripped hope from the hearts of my family.

True to ReVonda's prediction to the embassy liaison, they had arrived at the hospital almost exactly two hours following the phone call. They rushed through the halls trying to find me, only to encounter resistance. The hospital security officer refused to let them see me, making excuses and preventing them from going further. In full big sister protective mode, ReVonda challenged them full force, arguing and trying to convince the officer to let her see me.

Later she would tell me, "I acted a plum fool. We had gone all that way, and they wouldn't let me see you. I am not going to lie; I acted the fool. It took Greg a while to try to rein me in."

When the security officer informed ReVonda that he would have to call other security to help remove her if she didn't calm down, Greg and Uncle Lou escorted her into a waiting room to try to deescalate the situation and devise a plan.

The driver, Uncle Lou, had stayed with them at the hospital to help them make sure they were okay. He warned her that she was not going to help the situation if she pushed too hard and made a scene. He explained that since I was in intensive care, the hospital had highly restricted visiting hours, and it could be some time before ReVonda was allowed to visit.

Nonplussed, after a few minutes, ReVonda approached the security officer again and asked when they would be allowed to be let in. He told her that the doctors had informed him that they were not ready for me to be seen yet and that she would have to wait. Dissatisfied, she began another twenty-minute round of arguing and badgering the officer.

ReVonda wouldn't back down. She had to see me with her own eyes and make sure that I was alive and fighting. Finally, they agreed to let her go back and see me. I have a vague memory of seeing her burst through the doors and into my room. When she entered the room, she steeled herself for what she might find. Amazingly, my room was cool and clean compared to the desperate conditions of the rest of the hospital. This reassured her that at least they were making an effort to care for me.

Relief washed over her when she saw that my eyes were open and she knew without a doubt that I was alive. I think that she may not have fully believed it until that moment. She started a visual head-to-toe inspection of me, all the while trying to engage me in conversation to see if I was coherent. I was awake and talking but overwhelmed by pain and medication—I was anything but coherent. ReVonda continued her perusal of my condition, noting that my left leg was left uncovered by the blankets and appeared to be split open in some way. She calmly asked me while tenderly touching my foot, "Can you feel this?"

I groggily replied, "Yeah." I couldn't feel a thing, but my sluggish brain had noted her action and tried to respond in turn. She knew that I hadn't felt it but asked again.

"Can you feel this?" she repeated.

If I answered "yes," we both knew that I would be lying, so neither of us said anything. The room fell into an uneasy silence as Vonda surveyed the situation, assessing everything to put a plan of action into place. Overwhelmed by my condition and the heaviness of my grief, she was unsure how to help me find solace. She stood beside me, supporting me and giving me strength with her presence.

A doctor entered the room, and she immediately started quizzing him, "What's going on with my brother's leg?"

"We put it together as best we could, but it was missing pieces when he was brought in." The doctor looked uncomfortable as he spoke. "The whole leg didn't come in with him, so we had to use screws to try to put it together."

"Missing pieces? What do you mean his leg is missing pieces?" ReVonda couldn't process what she was hearing.

"We did the best we could," shrugged the doctor, his voice trailing away.

ReVonda struggled to make sense of what he was telling her. *Ti's leg was missing pieces? Surely, they could have done better than that.* As the doctor filed out, she began asking every nurse who entered the room as many questions as possible. They couldn't provide her with any answers aside from giving updates on my latest vitals, which were not good as my blood pressure continued to rise.

I don't remember ReVonda leaving the room and my mother coming in, but upon exchanging places, ReVonda left to update Greg and Uncle Lou, who were waiting in a small room nearby. As ReVonda gave them a report, Uncle Lou interrupted. He tried to explain that this was one of the nicest hospitals on the island and that the doctor who operated on my leg was an expert who had been brought in from the private hospital just for my surgery. ReVonda was having none of it.

"I have to disagree with you on that, Uncle Lou," she said. "I have seen nice hospitals before and not so nice hospitals—this is the worst hospital that I have ever been in." Although she appreciated his kindness and perspective, she wasn't taking my condition or the hospital's ability to properly treat me lightly. She knew that I needed better care or I would not survive.

Greg, ReVonda, and my mom huddled up to discuss what they had witnessed and to make a plan. They jointly decided that they needed to get me out of the hospital and take me to a facility where my care would be better. They started to advocate with the medical staff for this and were met with immediate resistance. The hospital staff assured them that they could adequately care for me and address my medical needs. My sister vehemently disagreed. She could see that I was deteriorating—my blood pressure continued to rise, and my leg, once wrapped post-surgery, was now open and exposed. ReVonda's faith in the doctor plummeted after he described the surgery on my leg, and she was appalled by the condition of most of the hospital. My family insisted that I be transported to better care in the United States; the hospital argued that they could not allow this. Locked in a frustrating stalemate, a woman named Claudette approached the group.

Claudette was some sort of liaison between the United States and the Bahamas, and her role had something to do with helping to stimulate tourism in the Bahamas. Respected in the community, she had knowledge, connections, and invaluable resources. Very polished and well versed in Bahamian protocols, it was evident that Claudette could bring guidance that my family was searching for as they worked to make decisions to improve my care.

Looking past the hospital administrators, Greg directed a blunt question toward Claudette, "Can you help us get him out of here?"

"Yes, I can do that," Claudette replied as my family turned their focus to her.

"We need to have him out of here within twenty-four hours," ReVonda emphasized. She and Greg had mutually concluded that if I were not moved within that time period, I would lose my leg, if not my life. They could see my body failing before their eyes. At that point, the hospital seemed more intent on sending in chaplains to discuss last rites than doctors to fight for life-saving treatment. Other people might be giving up on me, but ReVonda never would. If I couldn't fight for my life, she would fight for me.

Claudette provided them with two different numbers to call to start the ball rolling to get me moved. She emphasized that they wouldn't be allowed to take me anywhere unless they had my passports. Maleka and I had been staying on the island of Exuma, and I was now in Nassau, which presented a further problem. No one knew where my passport was or how to get it. Claudette helped guide my sister and Greg as they began making calls to determine the location of the passport. Eventually, they discovered that the island police held all of the belongings that Maleka and I had arrived with, including our passports.

Claudette drove ReVonda and Greg to meet with the police. They met them at the airport and would begin an exhausting process of arguing back and forth to get possession of my passport. The police didn't want them to take it, but they couldn't take me off the island without it.

ReVonda pleaded, "My brother is going to die if we don't get him off this island."

"I need to see Cameron grow
up. Please, God, let me live
to raise my son."

17

Race with Time

I lay in my hospital bed and watched my blood pressure continue to climb. Seeing ReVonda and my mom had brought me some comfort and relief in knowing that I was no longer on my own in the Bahamas. However, that did not make the difficulty of my reality any easier. My beautiful wife was still gone, and somehow, I had to gather the strength to tell my son, Cameron, before he heard the news from anyone else.

I couldn't imagine how I could possibly share the news with Cameron when I was still in shock myself, but I knew that it needed to be done. *How will I tell him? How do I say to him that the person he loves most in the world is never coming back? Lord, please help me and be with him.*

As I tried my best to gather strength for the call, I reached Maleka's dad by phone. He had already heard the news of her passing. Although he was heartbroken and devastated himself, conversing with him gave me assurance and peace. A pastor, he spoke to me with gentle, spiritual authority and explained that while Maleka was gone from earth, she was in a beautiful heavenly afterlife. Her purpose on earth was finished, but I had to carry on. Cameron had lost his mother, but he needed me to be there for him. He agreed to call Cameron with me and break the news to him together.

The call to Cameron was devastating. There was so much pain up to this point, but knowing that I was about to deliver soul-crushing news to my child was a pain unlike anything I had experienced. It was sheer agony. I tried my best to explain what happened; my voice choked with emotion as I pushed inadequate words out. I had no comfort to offer, just a deep void of pain and loss. Thankfully, Maleka's dad took over where I could not. He offered words of wisdom, comfort, and peace in an unimaginably difficult conversation.

I told Cameron, "I'm going to be okay," but I wasn't sure that my words held any truth. My blood pressure rapidly rose as the monitors changed from green flashing numbers to yellow. My heart rate was increasing, and my vitals were tanking.

God, please help me to be all right for my son. Please don't let me die, too. This is not fair. Why did you have to take Maleka? My son has already lost his mother; you can't take me away, too.

My faith in God began to wane. I couldn't understand why He would allow this to happen to us. Hadn't we followed His Word and been good stewards of all that He had given us? Surely, we didn't deserve to be punished in this way. How could a God who is supposed to be merciful and just allow this to happen?

I was filled with regret that I hadn't even seen Maleka before she passed. If the staff knew that she was dying in the clinic, why couldn't they have let me see her even if it was just to whisper a brief "I love you" to her? Nothing seemed right or fair, and this angered and grieved me.

After my call with Cameron, I lay alone in my room and watched my vitals change from bad to worse. The yellow lights were now flashing red. Something was seriously wrong. My blood pressure was 190/130, my heart rate was over 145 beats per minute, and my temperature was 104 degrees. My body was racked in pain, and I figured that I was going to die. The hospital sent in a priest to pray over me. The doctors issued orders and increased my medication, but nothing seemed to be making a difference.

Dear God, please don't let me die. I need to live. I need to be there for my son. Why did you keep me alive only to let me die in this hospital? What did I do wrong that you allowed this to happen to us? We didn't deserve death and suffering. Cameron does not deserve to have both his parents stripped from him. Please, Lord, let me

live. I need to live. I need to see Cameron grow up. Please,
God, let me live to raise my son.

As the machines around me flashed screams of red,
I fell into a disturbed sleep that I expected never to
wake from.

When I finally awakened, the machines' red flashes
had changed to yellow, and I was surprised to find that
I had survived the night. I knew that I was fortunate
to be alive, yet wary that there was still warring going
on as my damaged body raged with fever and relentless
pain. Whatever infection my body was fighting was a
fearsome foe.

My sister ReVonda came charging into my room.
Full of attitude, she declared, 'We are going to get you
the hell out of the hospital."

I had no idea of what ReVonda had been going
through while I was lying there. She had to fight to get
my passports, fight with police, fight with detectives,
fight to find me a way out of there. She made calls, had
meetings, investigated hospital options, spoke with
doctors, and pulled out any stop that she could think
of to ensure my survival. Greg and my mom battled
alongside her.

As they worked to get me out of there, it became
evident that the authorities intended to let me die on
the island. The hospital had been instructed to limit
the amount of treatment they were to give me; the

police had been directed to keep my passport and belongings, and policies were being issued to keep me from being airlifted out. Tourism was the island's primary industry, and the news continuing to spread about what had happened in the accident could rock the island's financial state. The clock was ticking for me, but an insidious undercurrent was trying to take my life. ReVonda wasn't about to let that happen.

In the midst of all that was happening, Maleka's body was brought to the hospital for identification. No one wanted that heartbreaking task, but my mom bravely stepped up to bear that burden. She confirmed what we already knew—Maleka was gone, and our lives had to carry on with the immense void of her loss.

Paramedics and an air ambulance arrived to transport me back to the United States but were immediately bogged down in red tape. My sister was ticked. She did not back down. She and Greg had committed to getting me out of there within twenty-four hours, and they would not be deterred. My family knew that Cameron would lose his father if I didn't get on that air ambulance. That outcome was not acceptable.

With Claudette's help, by that afternoon, the air ambulance was approved to take me. My mom and my sister were allowed to accompany me on the flight from Nassau, Bahamas, to a hospital in Fort Lauderdale, Florida. Greg was required to stay behind and answer questions from investigators, eventually catching a commercial flight into Florida. By 4:00 PM that afternoon, we had landed on U.S. soil. Within an hour of arriving, I was being checked and tested at the hospital and was given a thorough head-to-toe evaluation as they assessed all the damage from the blast, the inadequate treatment, and the infection that continued to rage.

My sister had asked Claudette to help her locate a top-level trauma center that could receive me in the United States. Claudette immediately took charge, arranging everything and lifting a huge burden off my sister. She made calls, spoke with various hospitals, and arranged for me to be transported to Broward Health Medical Center.

Through Claudette's efforts, one of the hospital administrators at Broward called my sister. "Ms. Hawkins, I have assembled the best trauma team in Broward County, and we are waiting and ready for whenever your brother arrives here."

He wasn't playing, either. When the air ambulance landed in Fort Lauderdale, the administrator was waiting. Dressed in a suit, he greeted my sister with a whole team of doctors and surgeons standing behind him. Not fully knowing the extent of all my injuries, he gathered anyone he thought might be needed to help save my life.

As I was being evaluated, one of the doctors took my sister and mom to the side and explained in a very calm and straightforward manner that they needed to allow the surgeons to do what was necessary to save my life.

"Do you mean that you are going to have to take his leg?" My sister asked.

"We don't know anything yet, but you are going to have to let us do what we need to do to save his life," replied Dr. Nichiporenko. He assured them that they had a specialist on the way to help make the determination.

The specialist, Dr. Merkel, was initially scheduled to do the surgery on my leg at a later time. When he examined it, he made the immediate decision that the leg would have to be removed and that this surgery needed to take priority over the other treatment that I needed to undergo. "If we don't take the leg, we will lose him," he determined.

My sister tried to reassure my mom. "We can lose his leg, but we can't lose Ti. We can get him another leg, but we can't get another Tiran."

My mom cried but acquiesced. "It's okay. I'm okay. Let's let them do what they need to in order to save his life."

I was wheeled into surgery, and the doctors did an outstanding job. In a terrible situation, they made the best choice they could to save my life.

"Shattered by loss
and battered physically,
how would I ever find
wholeness again?"

18

Life-Saving Surgery

A s I underwent surgery to remove my leg, my sister and my mom were well tended to by the hospital staff.

"They treated us like family," ReVonda recalled. There was so much going on, yet they made special efforts to treat my family with thoughtfulness and kindness.

The media had already gotten wind of my arrival and hounded the hospital for information. While I was in surgery, the staff liaison for communication approached my sister and asked her if she wanted to make a statement to the press.

She told the liaison that if the hospital needed to put out a statement, they could. She also firmly instructed him that she didn't want to talk to the press. All she and my mom wanted was to make sure that I would make it through this. She desperately wanted me to be safe and alive, and nothing beyond that mattered to her.

Exhausted and depleted from days of effort, working on my behalf, when the surgeons informed ReVonda and my mother that I had made it through surgery successfully, ReVonda fell on her knees and sobbed. All of the emotion she had pushed to the side to concentrate on saving my life streamed forth in a deluge of tears. Flooded with relief as the doctors assured her that I would be okay, she cried for the first time since hearing about the accident.

Amputation saved my life. However, this did not make waking up from surgery without part of my leg any less jarring. I had known that losing my leg was a probability, but now I faced a whole new realization. I was a broken man—physically, spiritually, and emotionally. Shattered by loss and battered physically, how would I ever find wholeness again? Still in a haze of shock, I was not ready to accept my circumstances.

ReVonda became my lifeline in the hospital. What do you even say to someone in circumstances like mine? Are there even words to encourage? Somehow, ReVonda instinctively knew what I needed. We cried together, we mourned together, and she coaxed out of me my feelings and fears for moving forward. The loss of Maleka was devastating, but I was also grappling with the loss of my entire existence as I knew it. How could I even be a man within the broken wreckage of my own body?

The surgery to remove my leg was one surgery in a series of many as doctors attempted to piecemeal me back together.

My left leg was gone but still needed an exacting follow-up surgery to position the bones so that I could walk with the help of a prosthesis one day.

My right foot was fractured—several of the bones were broken. A large, temporary pin that jutted out from my skin had to be placed to help structure the bones in my existing leg while it healed.

My collarbone was broken in four places and required surgical repair with a titanium plate and pins to stabilize it.

I had a fractured pelvis and a bruised rib on the lower left side. My L5 vertebra was chipped and fractured, and the risk of possible paralysis outweighed the benefit of potential surgery. These fractures were some of my more "minor injuries."

I had deep second-degree burns covering my right leg and burns on my right ear from where my skin had been on fire on the boat after the explosion. The burns extended through my epidermis and into the dermis and tissues below. It soon became apparent that I would need some significant skin grafts to help me heal. Instead of grafting from my own skin or that of a cadaver, the physicians chose to use skin grafted from a pig.

ReVonda tried to keep things as lighthearted as the situation could allow, calling me "pork rind" after the doctors harvested the pigskin to apply surgically to the site of my burns.

I tried to smile back at her jokes, but the accident had even altered my usually gleaming smile. One of my front teeth had been chipped. Seemingly minor, it was something that bothered me greatly. I had always taken great pride in my appearance, and although many of my injuries were not visible, this one was. It was frustrating that after all that my body had been through in the accident, I couldn't even smile without noticeable evidence of tragedy. It was as if my chipped tooth was taunting me every time I looked in the mirror, reminding me that my life would never be the same. Visually, this small reminder would continue to nag at me.

I had a series of grueling surgeries to fix, repair, and pin me back together. I joke now that my body contains more pins and screws than you will find in all of Home Depot. The reality was, though, that the surgeries were no joke. I was often in overwhelming amounts of horrendous pain as the doctors struggled to manage the extent of my injuries.

Most of my medical issues could be managed surgically, but some factors affected me mentally beyond my enduring grief. Not yet diagnosed, I had short-term memory loss, PTSD, and mental anguish in the form of deep depression.

I hadn't accepted my situation, but I couldn't avoid it, either. I knew how to manage life with Maleka by my side, but navigating it alone was a terrifying prospect. The thought of it was overwhelming. *How would life go on? How could I be a good father without her stabilizing support?*

I worried that I would never walk again. Doctors assured me that I could get a prosthetic, but that was at least six months down the road. Even with a prosthetic, how would I walk with fractured vertebrae and a broken "good leg"? I panicked when I thought about all the obstacles stacked against me. It seemed to be too much to overcome. Psychologically, I didn't know how to navigate all of the uncertainty I was facing.

"Each day, I drew strength

from her light by speaking to

her through my writing."

19

In Memoriam

During the initial days in the hospital, I was insulated, protected in a bubble by my sister, my mom, and Greg. They had watched over me, handled arrangements and decisions, and advocated endlessly for me. They kept the pressure of the outside world from me so that I could begin to heal.

Eventually, though, I became aware that other people were grieving. Beloved by so many, vigils, prayer services, and memorials had sprung up throughout the country to honor and remember Maleka.

I tried to watch a memorial service for Maleka on my laptop but had to shut it off. It was too real, too raw, too hard. The outpouring of love for my sweet angel was tremendous, but it was also difficult. It was beautiful to hear how much she meant to other people and the legacy that she left behind, but it was also hard to listen to others describe only small pieces of the woman that was my whole heart. No one could capture the essence, the strength, and the vivacious-ness of who I knew Maleka to be, and this hurt me somehow.

Used to talking through my problems with Maleka, I soothed myself by speaking to her through writing. I wrote a letter to be read by my friends and family, my words spilling out onto the page as I organized my thoughts and emotions.

Dear Family,

I want to let you know that my family and I are tremendously overwhelmed and gratified by the outpouring of love that has been shown during this tragedy. Even though I haven't been very responsive to anyone up to this point, I have read and reviewed many of the touching and inspira-tional words that you all have had for my family. These words have brought me strength and smiles during these extremely difficult times.

I've gone through so many emotional, mental, and spiritual challenges throughout trying to process what happened and why. I questioned why it wasn't me that the Lord took instead of Maleka. I would have gladly traded my life for hers. But I also know that God makes no mistakes, and it was time for Him to call her home. I'm very blessed to have come from this tragic incident with injuries that I should be able to recover from and get back to a somewhat normal life. However, I'm still grieving over the loss of losing the love of my life and having to face going forward without her physical presence here any longer.

Maleka. LoLo. Baby. MJ. Mrs. Jackson. Love of my life. All of these were names that I called her. Maleka was my queen and I would always refer to her as "my phenomenal, beautiful, wonderful wife." I worshipped the ground that she walked on, and she loved me in a similar fashion. She had a tremendous personality, love for life, love for our family, love for all she encountered, and love for the Lord. She was my best friend and such a great friend to so many. From her intelligence, wisdom, and great advice, her silly sense of humor and being a comedian on the sly, her being a great listener and not holding back her thoughts and opinions, to her animated facial expressions to her skills as an unlicensed bartender. Her beautiful voice and her love of singing, her silly smile and laugh, her love of cooking and providing for others, her love and parenting to our son, as well as her impact to other kids are just some of the ways she showed love. I could go on all day with this because she has been that much to me.

As everyone celebrates my wife from leaving us on this world to God's paradise in Heaven, please be in a joyous mood and continue reflecting about the fun and happy times that you've shared with her. Think about the smiles and joy that she brought to everyone. At times we take people for granted and the impact that they make on us. In my conversations with God, He's told me that it was time to focus and pay attention to the ways she made each of us here on earth better. This is the moment for that. He also thought it was time to bring his angel home so she could watch over more souls.

She has made me a better husband, father, God-fearing man, and a better person overall.

My life is changing in ways going forward that I never could have imagined or planned for. I'm still processing this and have an enormous level of grief, challenges that I am not even aware of yet, trying to be strong and help with this adjustment of this loss along with Cameron. I'm still fighting my injuries, but I'm improving heath wise, trying to finish up the surgeries I've been facing, and preparing for rehab. The mental and emotional pieces of this are still a greater challenge in me, but knowing the support that I have from you all is helping. I still have some spiritual rebuilding to do.

Thank you all once again for the love, strength, and contributions that you've made to help my family and me deal with all of these challenges *ongoing and ahead of us. Every one of you is a blessing to us. Please continue to pray for us.*

Maleka will always be with us in spirit. Rest in Heaven, my queen.

Writing this letter was cathartic and healing but simultaneously inadequate to express the depth of emotion and love I had for my wife and the gaping hole torn in my heart from her loss.

Each day, I drew strength from her light by speaking to her through my writing. I knew that she was no longer with me on earth, but the exercise of expression, typing out all the things I wanted to say to her, was a healing balm to my spirit. In writing, I could ask Maleka questions, tell her my fears, and find guidance for my journey. This instinctual action became a critical first step in releasing some of the survivor's guilt and torment that was building inside of me.

Part III

Resilience Resolve

"Resilience does not mean

regaining what was lost;

it means reshaping

what remains."

20

Reborn Resilient

I gulped in a breath as my body plunged below the surface of the chilly water. Even with the hot rays of the Alabama sun beating down on me, the cold clawed at my tiny body as I was drawn back upward, emerging from the surface with new life, reborn through baptism. I shivered as I stepped out of the water, my white robe clinging to my body.

At a summer revival when I was nine years old, I decided to give my life to Jesus. It was a choice that changed my life forever. Baptized in the Tennessee River, I was raised out of the water into a new life in Christ.

When I walked into the water, I had a choice. I could stay in the life I had been living or follow my convictions and be transformed. The former was safe and comfortable; the latter would be lasting. Unable to swim and scared of drowning, I stepped forward in faith and joined my Uncle Connie in the water. Buoyed by my uncle's solid frame and surrounded by the encouragement of friends and family members, I emerged from the water, reborn and renewed.

Over three decades later, as I lay in my hospital bed, sorrow threatening to drown me, I knew that I had a choice. I could choose to be swallowed up by the weight of my circumstances or I could be defiant in the face of death and loss, purposing to be resilient.

Resilience is a choice.

It is a conscious decision to keep moving forward against undeniable opposition. When I lost Maleka in the fiery waters of the boat explosion, all control was stripped away. I had to accept that tragedy occurred, but I did not have to let it triumph over me.

Responding with resilience means driving, pushing, pursuing—the determination that life will be better. Resilience does not mean regaining what was lost; it means reshaping what remains. Resilience is not a rescue or an easy road. It is the will to relinquish life forever altered and choose a new path with intention.

If something can crumble, that means that there remain materials left to rebuild. I felt as if my whole life had collapsed, but I knew that rebuilding was necessary, no matter how painful the process would be. Cameron needed me to be the best dad possible, which meant moving forward, even if it was one determined movement at a time.

It started with a small yet deliberate act. I shaved. Like weeds, whiskers had begun to cover my face with their unkempt overgrowth. A goatee had graced my face for as long as I had been married to Maleka, but as beard hairs overtook it, I decided that I needed a fresh start.

I asked for a mirror to be held in front of me, and there, in that hospital bed, I shaved all of my facial hair. I wasn't the same man I had been before the accident; I had to become something new. I chose to be reborn through an effort of resilience. I knew that it wouldn't be easy, but it was one roll of my wheelchair in the right direction.

My clean-shaven face represented a new beginning, but it didn't make things magically better. I was still trapped in a hospital bed, powerless to do such simple tasks as relieving myself without assistance. Since my injuries affected nearly every part of my body, I couldn't shift or get out of bed unless the hospital staff intervened, moving me, rolling me over, helping me relieve myself in a bedpan, or cleaning me. This was a new level of humbling, and I hated it.

The doctors determined that if I were careful and allowed myself to heal at a reasonable pace, I wouldn't need to have surgery on my spine or fractured pelvis. Healing naturally would put me at less risk for complications, but it didn't release me from my state of utter helplessness. As I lay in bed, a physical therapist walked into my room, pushing a wheelchair. My first movement toward independence appeared in the form of a wooden board. He carried a smooth plank, approximately two feet long by six inches wide. This simple slab was my ticket to freedom.

The challenge seemed easy. I was instructed how to position the board underneath myself so I could slide into the seat of the wheelchair. This would allow me the very basic dignity of transporting myself to the bathroom. I was eager to get started, but my eagerness quickly turned to exasperation as I tried, again and again, to accomplish the task without success. I couldn't use my shattered left shoulder to push, and my right arm was the only extremity mostly functional, but it grew fatigued after a few minutes of effort. ReVonda and my mom witnessed my struggle but knew that I had to learn to do this myself.

As I sweated and strained, I grew discouraged. I wanted to quit and languish in my misery but knew that this was not an option. The physical act of moving was difficult, but more importantly, I realized that I was scared. Fear had taken over.

Yes, I was in pain. Yes, I could barely move, but it was fear that was stopping me. I was afraid that if I did the task wrong, I would fall and hurt myself more. Fear outweighed my desire for freedom, and when I identified that, I knew that I had to fight harder. Over the next few days, my persistence paid off and the fear dissipated as I became more confident that I could move without falling.

Resilience means resisting obstacles that threaten to hold you where you are.

Moving into a wheelchair for regular use provided me with some encouragement. I could leave the confines of my hospital room and enjoy being pushed through the halls or meet with visitors in the family room where I could fellowship with Greg, my mom, ReVonda, or other visitors.

Once I made progress, this didn't mean that my physical and occupational therapists let me off the hook. They seized this victory as an opportunity to push me to achieve more, which is how I found myself with my back seated against a set of three or four stairs, tasked with sliding myself up them. Asking someone riddled with broken bones, covered in burns, and missing a leg to drag himself up these stairs backward felt akin to asking a newly mobile toddler to scale a mountain. It seemed impossible.

My right foot was in a cast. What remained of my left leg was also in a cast. For the purpose of this exercise, my left arm was useless and secured in a sling. I couldn't put any weight on either of my legs, and I was also attempting to navigate this entire situation with fractures in my spine and pelvis. A rigid brace protected my spine, which only made things more difficult. I pushed, sweated, struggled, cursed, and grew more and more frustrated by the endeavor. I knew that the staff was testing me both physically and mentally to determine my abilities and to prepare me to be able to leave the hospital, but I felt that it was a fruitless effort.

Resilience is knowing when rest is necessary for healing to take place. It is measuring resistance and choosing the wisest course of action.

I eventually accomplished the task in this case, but I felt the cost outweighed the gain. I needed to be able to complete basic tasks that allowed me to move, but I also needed to allow healing to occur so that I could attack those tasks with renewed vigor.

"At that moment, I knew that grabbing hold of life with passion and purpose was the only option for me."

21

Help and Healing

Physically I was battered and had lost significant weight, but I was making gradual strides toward improvement. Well, not literal strides as I was still wheelchair-bound, but I was definitely moving forward.

The hospital wisely continued to prepare me for when I would be ready to leave their care. As part of this, they sent a psychologist to regularly meet with me as I processed my loss, grief, and transition to caring for both Cam and myself. There was so much uncertainty that it was hard for me to reconcile what life would even look like without Maleka. Most days, I didn't want to confront that reality, but I knew that I had to for healing to take place. I also knew that my recovery would directly affect Cameron, which motivated me to pursue that with purpose.

Mentally and emotionally, I was devastated, and part of me wanted to wallow in that for a while. I was angry at God and was grappling with survivor's remorse. Maleka was a much better person than I was, and it didn't seem fair that God took her instead of me out of the two of us. Her earthly impact was far more significant than mine; she should have been the one to live. I had a tablet with me in the hospital, and I began to read through Scripture on it to try to make sense of the nature of God and why He allowed this tragedy to occur.

As I scrolled through the Bible, I read Romans 8:28 (NIV): "And we know that in all things God works for the good of those who love Him, who have been called according to His purpose." Maleka loved God, and hadn't she been called according to His purpose? If so, why had she died while I remained? I thought that I loved God but was pretty angry at Him. How could He possibly work any of this situation out for good? What was good about a mother being ripped away from her son? What was good about devastating loss, pain, and injury? If God supposedly worked all things to our good and His glory, what was He doing in this disaster? Where was the good? I choked back sobs as I raged at God.

Comfort came in the form of someone deeply entwined in their own grief. Maleka's dad hadn't just helped me break the terrible news to Cameron, but he also walked beside me in my valley of despair. He put his pain aside to counsel me, naturally assuming his mantle for pastoral care. I wanted to know the why. *Why God? Why Maleka?*

Maleka's dad advised that the "why" was not important. We didn't need to know the why but only trust that God did and He was faithful. I wasn't so convinced—God didn't seem very faithful or trustworthy in that situation, and I demanded an explanation.

Her dad patiently reasoned with me. He told me that Maleka was in Heaven where she had eternal life—this far outweighed any earthly experience that this life could have offered her. I knew this to be true. I knew that if anyone was in Heaven, it was Maleka. I had no doubts or questions about that. She loved the Lord deeply and lived a profoundly purpose-filled life.

Her dad explained that Maleka's faith had prepared her for this moment—that we will all die eventually, and that this was Maleka's time. Perhaps her impact on everyone had been monumentally significant because her time on earth was so brief. I also recognized this to be true. Maleka's faith had prepared her for Heaven, yet she hadn't held back in leaving an impact while she was alive. She had lived with enthusiasm and purpose and left a lasting legacy.

I also saw that I could have died three times, and God kept me on earth for a reason. I could have died in the explosion, I could have died in the hospital in the Bahamas, and I could have died from any one of the surgeries in Florida—yet I was still here. God must have orchestrated that for a purpose. I couldn't yet see that purpose, but I was beginning to acknowledge that some of these things required me to grasp trust in the Lord in a way that challenged me.

I knew these things to be true, but I also knew that my faith was shaken in a way that I had never experienced before. I had known grief before, especially when my dad had passed away a few years prior, but I hadn't known these depths of devastation. Maleka's dad's message resonated with me, but I wanted to reject it. I wasn't ready to release the anger that I held. I wasn't prepared to let God off the hook. My anger wanted answers, but instead, God gave me comfort in the care and fellowship of others.

The Lord also gave me an unlikely gift in the form of a television show. Frustrated by my slow rehabilitation progress and my utter helplessness, I grappled with feelings of futility. It was evident that life would never be the same, but being alive and living aren't really the same thing. God had kept me alive, but what if my quality of life were such that I couldn't truly live? Distraught and discouraged, these thoughts played on repeat in my head. My body was maimed and broken—how could I function in my condition?

As my mom sat in vigil at my bedside, we turned on the television show *American Ninja Warrior*. I had watched the show a few times but wasn't an avid consumer. Watching healthy, athletic men and women defeat incredible physical challenges hardly seemed the thing to boost my mood, yet for some reason, I stopped and watched anyway.

As I watched, a young man named Zach Gowan stepped up to the podium to compete. Smiling, he raised both arms to the sky before reaching down to unfasten something at his waist. Within moments, he removed a prosthetic leg, lifting it above his head in celebration. The crowd went wild! As he hopped in place, I observed skeptically, uncertain of what someone with only one leg could accomplish on an athletic event of such magnitude. Grinning, he set about the task of completing the obstacles. His expression shifting to determination, he hopped—*no, leaped!*—from obstacle to obstacle.

The announcer exclaimed, "While cancer took his leg, it can't take his heart—his heart or his will! Unbelievable!"

Challenges that had eliminated other potential warriors, Zach overcame—just in a different way. The crowd buzzed with excitement chanting "Zach! Zach! Zach!" as they roared every time he made it through a stage of completion.

When he finally fell, it was with a flourish, and the audience gave him a boisterous ovation with some spectators so touched and inspired by his actions, they wiped tears from their eyes. My own reaction was intense and immediate. If this young man could defeat cancer and live life with one leg with strength and intensity, I could grasp the gift of life with the same surety. At that moment, I knew that grabbing hold of life with passion and purpose was the only option for me. This was the course that I needed to take. This was my way forward.

"We are made stronger when
we are buttressed by the
strength of others."

22

Tribe of Transition

Determining and doing are two different things. I knew that I needed to pursue a path of resilience, but practically this proved very hard to accomplish.

As I continued to come to grips with everything that I was dealing with, my family remained my most substantial support. My mom, ReVonda, Greg, and family members and friends gave me messages of love and encouragement. I knew that I wasn't the only one grieving, but grief is a curious thing. We share loss, but grief is an individual journey. We each struggle to process things in our own way and on our own time-line. Some find solace at the very moment that others are overwhelmed in mourning. We don't choose when grief will grip us or when joy will emerge. I am eter-nally grateful that in the midst of their grief, so many people poured out their love on me.

While Maleka's dad acted as my spiritual advisor, ReVonda was my support and closest confidant. She spent hours and hours by my side—just being there. She sat with me, cried with me, laughed with me, and listened to me. We told stories and shared tears, and we started to map out a plan for the future.

Resiliency is choosing to evaluate current circumstances and make a plan for growth. Physically I was growing stronger, and my time in the hospital was nearing an end. I needed a plan in place to rehab so that I didn't have to be cared for 24/7, and I also needed to be near Cameron.

ReVonda helped me to begin to explore possibilities. We started working with a next steps coordinator to figure out where I could go to recover. ReVonda suggested that I go to Vanderbilt University Medical Center since it was near her in Nashville, Tennessee. This seemed to be a great option as it would allow me to rehab in-hospital so that I wouldn't have to rely on family or friends to take care of me, yet I could still be close to them for visits and encouragement. I thought that if I recovered enough there, I could get to where I was able to use crutches and be less dependent on other people. From my prior Achilles and knee injury experiences, I had learned that rehab was essential. However, I also knew that there was a lot that someone could do while on crutches. I just needed to get to this point and out of the wheelchair stage.

Even then, I knew that recovery would still be arduous with all of my injuries. However, I figured that if I transferred to Vanderbilt until I was more mobile, I could go back to Atlanta and have my mom help care for Cameron and me for a while.

Days passed before we heard back from Vanderbilt. We were confident that they would accept me but just needed the green light to move forward in our plans. Finally, we got a reply. They rejected me because my right arm was the only extremity that could fully function. Vanderbilt didn't think they were equipped to deal with someone with the magnitude of injuries I had. This denial of care shocked me, and it felt hurtful. I didn't think that they would turn away someone that needed help. I understood their perspective, but it still stung on top of everything else I was going through.

I didn't want to be a burden to anyone, yet it was apparent that I needed to rely on others, or I would never be able to recover enough to care for myself and Cameron. Thankfully, ReVonda stepped in for the rescue again.

She and Greg insisted that I come to stay with them until I was more mobile on my own. They began making arrangements and talking to friends in the medical community who could help. Thankfully we discovered that my insurance covered in-home care, treatment, and therapy. The plan was to be transported there by air ambulance for my next recovery phase.

Like the other air ambulance rides, the one to Nashville was horrific. Stuck on my back with less than a foot between my face and the ceiling of the craft, I felt sickened by claustrophobia as the ride buffeted us with turbulence. I lay there silently sweating, my skin growing clammy as I anxiously prayed to land soon.

Once in Nashville, things were already in place for my arrival. ReVonda arranged for equipment for my care to be brought in, and health care worker visits were scheduled. Everyone was as prepared as possible for this next phase, although we all underestimated just how difficult the transition would be.

I was still mostly immobile. I was also in a tremendous amount of pain, yet I wanted to ease off the pain medications as soon as possible. Beginning this process transitioned me into an even more difficult healing challenge.

As I slowly weaned off medications, sleep became disrupted. I would fall asleep only to wake up sweat-soaked in a gasping panic. *Maleka!* I could feel the fire, smell the smoke singeing my nostrils, and I was lost in the terror of being back there in real-time. It was terrifying. Over and over, the events of the accident burned my brain whenever I closed my eyes. I needed sleep, but going to sleep meant waking in a PTSD-induced panic. It was horrific. I couldn't escape the haunting images that screamed in my head. Every moment felt as if I were reliving the gruesome events of that day.

Sometimes we find ourselves in a season of life where we are stuck. Overwhelmed by life's circumstances, we find ourselves paralyzed with fear. Frozen in this fear, each decision or step forward seems impossible. We are trapped by the weight of our inaction, fighting to function as the world keeps moving around us.

Being stuck is often our bodies' response to trauma. Unlike flight or fight, the freeze mechanism takes over in a prickling of anxiety, trapping us in place and rendering us immobile. Our brains become foggy as we try to fight to slog through even the simplest of tasks. We know that we need to move forward, to keep going, yet we feel weighted in place. For some, being stuck is simply a season, a plateau in an otherwise forward-moving life, but others stay stuck in a long-term cycle of freeze as their bodies entrap them through depression, anxiety, or chronic pain and illness. This disabling disassociation is made for our protection from trauma, but when it becomes permanent, it becomes a trauma itself as it prevents us from ever healing and moving forward.

The state of being stuck is a place of inaction, and action needs to take place to counteract it. This seems both obvious and counterintuitive. How can we move forward when we are stuck? In life, we may not have control over our circumstances, but we always have a choice. Sometimes the choice is simply to inhale the next breath, take the next step, or do the next thing.

This stuck state is eventually where I found myself. I had determined to continue forward, yet I was battling psychological stress that kept me firmly fixed in place. Physically, I was dependent on everyone else. Psychologically, I was unraveling on a level that I couldn't control. Emotionally, I was drowning in the deepest depths of pain and heartbreak. I needed a lifeline.

Fortunately, I was surrounded by a tribe of supporters who would not allow me to be stuck. ReVonda and Greg led my team of caretakers, given that I resided in their home. ReVonda nurtured me physically, mentally, and emotionally through a phase jokingly described by her as the period of time when "a grown man became a giant baby." I disagree with her characterization, but the fact is that season was rough. She spent hours upon hours caring for me, crying with me, and talking through every possible aspect of my situation's outcome. She spoke to me as a man instead of a little brother and encouraged me that one day life would resume, and like the American Ninja Warrior that I had seen on TV, I would regain all that I had lost—just in a different way.

ReVonda was determined that I wouldn't waste away wallowing in sadness. She was an efficient and demanding taskmaster. Every day she made me get up and get out of bed. She would open the blinds to my protestations and declare, "Okay, it is time to get up and get in your wheelchair." She wasn't insensitive to my loss, but she was insistent on my healing.

Once out of bed, she would wheel me into the other room, where I would use the wooden board to slide into the recliner. That small change of environment helped me to feel tiny sparks of normalcy. We watched TV there, talked, scheduled appointments, and made arrangements with the insurance company. I maintained my journaling habit, and my friend and fraternity brother, Chris Jones, hooked me on audiobooks about entrepreneurship. Everyone around me was determined to help keep me moving, even on the days when I longed to envelop myself in darkness and despair.

ReVonda's house became host to a team of medical care workers whose task was to tend to me and rehab me. I struck up a camaraderie with many of them, and at some point, ReVonda became convinced that they were there not only to take care of me but also because they liked hanging out with me. They helped boost my spirits by talking to me as friends, without pity, and with encouragement and motivation. These interactions helped to keep me from being too much in my head and diving back into my deepest lows.

I innately learned that to some extent, I could manage those moments of intense emotional pain where the cold, foreboding fist of grief grabs my heart from nowhere and squeezes until I am spent with the sadness of it all. I realized that although I cannot control grief, I can respond to it differently. When I started to feel its grip, I would steady myself through distraction—whether through conversation, physical therapy, or the latest Netflix release. I could avoid getting stuck in a painful spiral by feeling all the feel-ings—just in a more measured way. I moved slowly through the sadness, trying to avoid being completely engulfed in it. With the help of my tribe, professional counseling, and strategies for coping, I was able to creep slowly forward in my recovery.

When I was a boy, I was determined to leave the small-town life I knew behind me. In these new circumstances, I realized that once again, I had to have a plan to move forward, or I would never survive. In the hospital, my goal had been primarily to stay alive. In this new phase of recovery, I knew that I had to accept the help and care of others humbly. I needed to rely on what I came to term as my "Tribe of Transition." Whether a person has experienced an immense trauma as I had or is experiencing personal upheaval such as divorce, job upheaval, the loss of a friendship, a business venture failing, or any number of difficult experiences, that person's tribe becomes essential. We can handle only so much on our own, and when we are experiencing hardship, we will often desire to hide away in reclusive behavior, but this is not to our benefit. We are made stronger when we are buttressed by the strength of others. Relying on the strength of others for a respite amid transition is a crucial marker in the choice of resilience.

When we are brave enough to accept help humbly, it creates a beautiful synergy around us. We learn the value of others and recognize the gifts that they bring to the table. Learning to ask for help when needed is an intensely vulnerable experience, but it harvests much growth. Having the strength to stand alone is important, but being smart enough to know when to ask for help is essential.

Relying on my tribe propelled my healing process. I rehabbed with intensity and focus, and the team around me accepted nothing less. I knew from my previous injuries that recovery was hard work, so I realistically tempered my expectations. I didn't expect healing to happen overnight. I knew it would be a long journey, but I could rely on my tribe when things got too difficult.

"Even in Maleka's death, the Lord was magnified as God used her story to touch and transform the hearts of many."

23

Cameron

The first time Cameron saw me after the accident was upon my return to Nashville. I was doing my best to settle into my new situation yet was obviously in a tremendous amount of discomfort. I was propped up in a recliner with my wheelchair positioned close by when Cam entered the room. He silently took in my altered appearance, my various bandages, and my missing leg. I had a brace on what was left of my missing leg, wrapped to promote healing and prevent infection where the amputation had occurred. I had a cast on my right foot that covered up to my calf. I also was strapped into a bulky back brace. My tooth was chipped, and my hair was singed. Grafts of pigskin covering burns comprised parts of my skin. I had lost about twenty-five pounds since the accident. Physically, I looked shockingly broken.

My appearance must have been jarring for Cameron. The weight of his grief appeared heavily on him, and it was excruciatingly evident that he was hurting emotionally. Viewing my injuries caused him even more pain. He sat quietly in a chair near me as we tenderly carved out our first tentative moments together without Maleka. It was heartbreaking. Cameron looked torn between relief that I was there talking to him and terror that I could be taken from him in an instant. I don't think my shattered appearance alleviated his fears. I knew that it was startling to see me as I was, but I was confident that we would find a way forward.

Apprehension marred his sweet face as we began awkward, stutter steps toward renewing meaningful conversation.

"How are you doing, Dad?" Cameron asked tentatively.

I struggled to answer honestly, feeling that any answer that I gave would be inadequate.

"How are you able to sleep?" he questioned, concerned, viewing a large support wedge on my bed in the other room.

I replied as best I could. Then I asked him some simple questions to distract him from my condition. "How are things staying at TJ's house?" Maleka's brother Shan had a son named TJ, and Cameron stayed with them while we were in the Bahamas and during the subsequent aftermath of the accident.

Our conversation continued, "How's the dog? Are you taking good care of Indiana?"

I was so happy to see Cameron, but I could tell that it was uncomfortable for him to see me so damaged. It was awkward for me, too, as I sensed that this version of me was a stranger to him.

Eventually, our conversation fell into a pregnant silence as we both mutely stared at the TV. There was so much to express, yet neither of us was prepared for a conversation brimming with desolation.

This scene replayed in short stints several times with some minor improvements as we began to navigate our new normal. It was a long time before we had a straightforward conversation about Maleka or the accident, but when we did, it centered on her not being there. We both keenly felt a deep void from her absence. Maleka had such a strong presence in life that everything seemed faded and dim without the brightness of her light.

I began to make plans for Maleka's funeral. Cameron didn't want to go, and on the day of the funeral, when it came time to view Maleka's body, it was understandably too much for him. Maleka's cousin Brittany stepped in to take him to a hotel and water park to distract him and help him manage his own emotions as the rest of us joined in celebrating Maleka's life.

In navigating retrieval of Maleka's body back from the Bahamas, I had been able to view the autopsy report. Maleka had fought to live for two hours post-accident, ultimately succumbing to massive amounts of hemorrhaging. The damage to both of her legs was so extensive that she would have lost them both, and she would have been paralyzed. She also had internal damage to her kidneys, liver, and other organs. Had she survived, her quality of life would have been impossible to regain. In a sad way, this knowledge gave me solace. It helped me to know that she was in Heaven and was not suffering here on earth. This knowledge didn't make her loss any less painful, but it did bring me some peace.

The funeral was held less than a week after I arrived at ReVonda's, and I was not physically, mentally, or emotionally prepared for it. The services were held in Chattanooga, Tennessee, two hours away from ReVonda's house. My friend Chris Jones flew in to help ReVonda and Greg care for me during the funeral and the travel. His presence was a comfort as he helped push my wheelchair and care for my safety. Physically, the travel and hotel stay were exhausting. I still had to use a wooden board to transfer from my wheelchair to a car or seat, and movement was exceedingly painful.

The trip and events weren't just difficult for me; my supporters were struggling with managing their own emotions. On the day of the visitation, ReVonda was having a hard day, while I seemed to be having a manageable day. She was tired, stressed, and emotionally spent. ReVonda struggled to help me into a suit she had purchased for the occasion and then nearly burst into angry tears when she realized she had forgotten to buy me shoes.

"Dammit! I forgot the shoes." Her usually upbeat voice quavered.

"What am I going to do with some shoes?" I said teasingly, nodding toward where my foot used to be, and where my other foot remained bound in a cast.

At that moment, the tension that was gathering released as we melted into laughter. Sometimes dark humor is needed to add some levity to a difficult situation.

When the day of the funeral came, I was not ready emotionally. I still was processing Maleka's loss and to have to be comforting people in theirs was beyond my capacity. I wasn't prepared to say goodbye, and I definitely was not ready to process things in such a public setting. I was operating largely in survival mode, and the day's sorrow seemed unbearable.

Since the accident occurred, I had given strict instructions to ReVonda that I didn't want my picture taken. I didn't want to see myself physically broken, and I wasn't steeled to fully accept what had occurred. In time, I would be, but mentally I needed to ease into things. This pertained to my leg, too. I didn't want to look at the angry scar where the amputation occurred and refrained from doing so when my bandages were changed. I still needed a little piece of denial to help ease me into acceptance.

On the day of the funeral, any personal preservation methods that I had tried to maintain were shattered. I wanted to observe the services and mourn my beloved wife quietly, but I felt like a spectacle that day. Attendees pushed for hugs without regarding my physical state; gawkers tried to snap selfies or photos with me—internally, I was seething. I knew that people were glad to see me safe, but I was distraught at the insensitivity and lack of tact or respect. I didn't want to pose for photos with my broken-toothed smile and shattered heart. I was grieving, and I didn't want it documented in photos or on social media. Chris and ReVonda stepped in as unofficial bodyguards. They pushed people away and tried to preserve my peace as best as possible.

I know that people were not trying to be intentionally hurtful. The church was packed with friends and family, which was evidence of how loved both Maleka and I were. However, I looked broken. I felt broken. I didn't want to be reminded that I was broken. I needed sensitivity and compassion. I had determined that I was going to be better, that I was going to become stronger, and that I would honor Maleka by rebuilding my future and my life. I didn't want reminders of how far away I was from my goals. I needed a vision of what

I could accomplish and how I would achieve a resilient life for myself and Cameron.

My tribe of supporters once again came through for me. ReVonda, Greg, Chris, my mom, and so many others reminded me that even though Maleka was gone, I was still here on earth for a reason.

Maleka's dad continued ministering to me, hammering the verse Romans 8:28 (NIV) into my head over and over: "And we know that in all things God works for the good of those who love him, who have been called according to his purpose." I think that he knew that I needed to take this verse to heart to move forward. I needed to imprint on my heart that God was working for my good and His glory, and that the Lord had a plan and purpose for my life that was not to be squandered.

Although heartbreaking, the funeral was a further reminder of how significant Maleka's impact had been on this earth. It was evident that her faith and the loving way she lived her life had left a legacy for others. Even in Maleka's death, the Lord was magnified as God used her story to touch and transform the hearts of many. Through memorializing and celebrating Maleka's life, the glimpses of God working sustained me and gave me the courage and motivation to carry on.

"If the pain of what I had endured could encourage others, God was using my story for good. "

24

Healing Steps

One day, I shakily pulled myself to a stand in front of a mirror. I hadn't wanted to look at myself or see what I had become, but I needed to. I needed to accept what had occurred to continue to move forward fully. I took a deep breath and faced my reflection. As much as I had relied on my tribe to help me transition through the survival phase, I ultimately needed to return to self-reliance to thrive. My tribe would still be there for me, but the roles would change. I re-evaluated where I was and made a plan for where I needed to be. I had to release the anger I held at God and realize the direction that the Lord was leading me in. The life that I had known was gone forever, but God was helping me to forge a new path.

Once again, I silently reminded myself of Romans 8:28 (NIV): "And we know that in all things God works for the good of those who love him, who have been called according to his purpose." I had been reading this verse repeatedly, meditating on it until I began to believe it and fully take it to heart. As I read God's Word and came to understand it, my anger began to melt away. The words resonated with me as I saw them revealed in my life.

Physically, I had started to make great strides (this time literally). I moved from a wheelchair to crutches and finally transitioned to learning how to walk with a prosthetic. As I healed, I stunned the doctors with the speed of my recovery.

The time that I spent rehabbing at ReVonda's was invaluable. She and the entire team around me had pushed me forward again and again. ReVonda had helped me physically, learning how to dress my wounds, stimulate the nerves at the sight of my amputation, and helping me learn to be more independent in my daily function.

She had also carried me emotionally when I wasn't strong enough to process the weight of Maleka's loss. ReVonda listened, laughed, teased, pushed, cajoled, and basically became my personal superhero. She was a constant positive reminder that life moves forward, whether we are prepared or not. She hadn't planned for all of this either, yet amid her own busy schedule and the stress of caring for me, she still executed her responsibilities in life with excellence and fortitude. Her love for me was sacrificial and like a healing balm to my heart. She always knew when it was time to speak or time to sit in grief beside me.

ReVonda understood that the seemingly little things, such as getting my chipped tooth fixed, were big as far as building my confidence, and she helped facilitate them. She wanted me to stay with her long term and for Cameron to join us, too, but she recognized that for me to feel whole again, I needed to relearn to rely on myself and be the man and father that Cameron needed me to be. So, once again, she helped me plan my next course of action.

I needed to move back to Atlanta. This was the city that Cameron and I called home, and we needed to restore what we could from our life there. In ReVonda's absence, my mom graciously agreed to move in with Cameron and me until we felt stable and could make it independently. I appreciated the continued sacrifices that my family and Maleka's made to ensure our future.

Cameron struggled to return home. At first, he did not want to be in the house, and I more than understood. Being there reminded us more sharply that Maleka was absent, and it would be some time before we both sorted through these emotions.

I made it a priority to establish grief counseling for both Cameron and me. I knew that we would both need emotional and mental support and guidance in the years forward. I did not see this as a short-term treatment but a long-term relationship with mental health care. I knew that there's often a stigma surrounding men seeking mental health help, and I didn't want Cameron ever to feel deterred by this. I wanted him to be assured that consistent mental health care is as vital as physical rehab and that healing needed to be a holistic, all-encompassing endeavor.

As we transitioned back into life in Atlanta, God once again showed us His faithfulness through a network of friends and helpers that pitched in to help us adjust and stabilize. I began to seek out the mentorship of my pastor, Keith Norman, who reaffirmed the lessons that God was already teaching me.

Spiritually, I was growing stronger. Emotionally, I was turning a corner, but it was a two-step forward, one step back process as grief maintained its grip on me. I had to learn to accept that grief would always be present. Acknowledging this helped me understand and function in my new normal. Knowing that grief was a constant companion in life helped me live my life more intentionally and not be caught off guard when a surge of sadness poured over me. Grief was inevitable and undeniable evidence of how loved Maleka was.

Physically, I was continuing to defy the odds. Fitted with a prosthetic, I had gone from walking to starting to run on an anti-gravity treadmill. It was a treadmill designed to keep weight and pressure off of my prosthetic until both of my legs proved strong enough. Eventually, I would gain the strength to run on my own.

Choosing resilience didn't mean Maleka was forgotten—on the contrary, she was the driving force that propelled me forward. I wanted to honor her memory by living life with a purpose and a passion, being the best parent to Cameron that I could be. As Cameron and I adjusted to life without Maleka, we learned a new father-son way of living life and relating. Maleka had always been central to our dynamic, but we had to adjust and change course. I resumed coaching Cameron and supporting him in his art and sports, but I also came to realize that my role as his father was far more critical in his teen years than I ever imagined. I was challenged to be a strong male role model for him to heal and thrive alongside me. We often moved at different paces in our healing journeys. Still, the important thing was that we were present for each other and supported each other, motivating the other toward growth just as Maleka had done so many times in the past for us both.

No one could ever replace Maleka, but we could honor her memory and the way that she lived her life by living our lives fully and with intention. We could choose a course of resilience, resisting relapsing into despair by surrounding ourselves with the strength of our supporters and a plan for the future.

Many times during my recovery, people had encouraged me with the verse, Jeremiah 29:11 (NIV): "'For I know the plans I have for you,' declares the

Lord, 'plans to prosper you and not to harm you, plans to give you hope and a future.'" I had read it but hadn't been ready to internalize or receive it until one day when I got a call from a friend who had helped work with me in my prosthetic process.

A gentleman who wasn't much older than I was had stepped on a nail, and the resulting infection was about to cost him his foot. Even though he knew in advance that he would lose his foot, he was terrified and discouraged. My friend Shane asked me to visit him and talk to him. I met with him and encouraged him that life wasn't over when you became an amputee. I shared my story with him and tried to leave him with some inspiration that his recovery could be remarkable and that his new prosthesis didn't have to slow him down in life. I explained to him the agony of my own journey, yet also gave him hope as I had reached a point where athletically, I was able to achieve almost everything that I had been doing pre-accident. Miraculously, even after all the injuries I endured, I was no longer in physical pain other than middle age's everyday aches and fatigue.

We connected, and the exchange encouraged him, but it also altered me. It was after that meeting that I realized that God was "working all things together for good" and "that He did have plans to give me a hope and a future." If the pain of what I had endured could encourage others, God was using my story for good. There was a beautiful and brilliant hope in that.

"I can share my story,

my struggles, and my tragedy

in the hope that they bring

healing and direction

to other people."

25

Life Will Never Be the Same

The Christmas after the accident, I couldn't move. I was so sad that I stayed in one spot. Maleka's family would come to visit in a typical year, and she would cook food for all of us. The house would hum with people and Maleka's vibrant spirit. She was always at the center of the celebration, and her absence felt unbearable. Traditions fell apart as I fell apart. Life with Maleka was vivid and dynamic, but the house now felt muted, empty.

Cameron was struggling, too. Maleka made holidays magical. She transformed the house as she decorated, singing and dancing with Cameron. We would share eggnog and laughs as we reveled in the joy of the holidays. All of that joy seemed lost without her.

Cameron and I were healing and working hard to build new traditions, but I felt as if I had nothing to give that Christmas. Grief once again gripped me and tried to hold fast. Without my tribe around me, I had to pull myself out of it. The strength that I had gained from others was absent; I now had to stand on my own. This realization was one of the hardest in my relationship with resilience.

I hadn't ever planned on being a single parent, and I struggled to make sense of my own changing emotions. I found myself hyper-vigilant regarding Cameron, trying to determine the difference between normal teenage reactions and behaviors resulting from losing his mom tragically. We were both grappling with the process of grieving, accepting, and starting to move forward. I knew how difficult things were for me, and Cameron also needed help. This is why I had been so adamant about getting us both into counseling. He had lost his mom, and I so desperately wanted to fill that void for him, but I couldn't. I could never make up for Maleka's loss. The only thing I could control was improving myself and hoping those changes impacted Cameron.

Maleka seemed to have always been a part of me, and I was dependent on her in such a way that I lost myself in us. It took work to learn who I am on my own and not be enmeshed in who we were versus who I am. It is magical when you have that soul-deep connection with someone, but it is terrible when it is stripped away. I felt lost, rudderless—I didn't know who I was without her. Horrible things birthed a new beginning. The rebirth was painful, difficult, and uncomfortable, but it was necessary for life to thrive.

I learned to accept things for what they are while knowing that, in time, there will be change, growth, and healing. Maleka had lived life beautifully in her time, but God had allowed that time to come to an end. Maleka completed her job on earth, but we all still have work to fulfill until we are called to Heaven one day.

If you had asked me before the accident what my purpose was, my answer would have been vague, a muddled understanding of the goodness that God had in store for me. I would have probably said that my purpose was to be a great dad and husband, to do well at my job, and to give back to my community.

If you had asked Maleka what her purpose was, she knew it, clear as day. She would have said that her purpose was to be a shining light, to help other people discover their own purpose, and to guide them on their journey. She knew her calling in Christ and lived her purpose fully and with intention every single day. She was relentless in fulfilling what God called her to do. She helped other people gain direction, leading them and helping them make sense of their lives, finding fulfillment in all they did. Maleka had tremendous discernment, and people sought her out for advice and encouragement. She helped friends, family, strangers—it didn't matter who they were; she used her gifts to inspire and motivate.

Like a beacon shining through the darkness, Maleka's light reached through the murky uncertainty of what I thought my life's work should be. In her passing, she showed me that I had a much greater purpose than I had ever imagined. Her final gift to me was to reveal that I could no longer sit by and settle for simply passing at being good at life. Good was no longer good enough. I had been given a grander calling, a purpose in God far beyond myself and my capabilities. With the Lord's leading, a new life was revealed as my pain gave birth to purpose.

An athlete sitting on the bench is given a job. Their job is to watch the game and prepare, studying the person playing their position and learning from their successes and failures. When the player on the field or court is injured, a substitution has to be made, and the player on the bench is propelled forward, challenging them to rise to the position that they have been placed in.

Life with Maleka was like that. She played and participated in life as if she were on the first string—as if every moment mattered and every decision needed to be made with her best intention. She poured her whole heart into everything that she did, holding nothing back. Since she was such a brilliant player, I could sit on the bench. I was part of the team but was able to observe. My participation was important, yet it was more of a passive role. I admired her and learned from watching her. It was easy to be an observer—to be good enough to be on the team without fully playing the game.

When Maleka was called home, it was as if I were suddenly pulled off the bench as a substitute for our team's best player. I floundered at first. I didn't know how I could fill her role or do mine. I didn't want to let my team down (Cameron, my family, Maleka's family, our friends, etc.), but I had no choice. Our star player was out of the game, and I had to step up and stand strong (even if it was on only one leg). Subconsciously, I started to implement some of the same things that she had faithfully done, yet in my own unique way. I couldn't fill Maleka's shoes, but I had learned from her and had been guided by her, and I knew that it was my job to pick up her mantle.

My calling and purpose do not look exactly like Maleka's, but it is the same at the core. It is to help people and guide them to make sense of their lives when they face hardship. I help others find their purpose through their pain. I can share my story, my struggles, and my tragedy in the hope that they bring healing and direction to other people. Even in death, Maleka remains a shining light to me.

"I choose not to let adversity and hardship triumph over me; instead, I resolve each day to live with resilience."

Epilogue

I have shared my story many times in the years following the accident. I have had the privilege of speaking at conferences, at events, on podcasts, and in the media. The first time I shared my message to a group of listeners, my voice wavered and broke with emotion as I imparted the impact of my experience.

With practice and the passage of time, my message has become stronger and more measured. Speaking about unimaginable loss and tragedy is always difficult due to the emotions it evokes, but my pain bears a purpose.

Why do I share a message that is so deeply personal and agonizingly vulnerable? I share it so that others who struggle will find hope, inspiration, and healing. Whether we recognize it or not, our life experiences have uniquely prepared us for whatever challenges or trials arise. There is life after loss, and we must choose to live it well. If I can survive my circumstances, you can thrive in yours.

Once a busy engineering executive, I now am an investor, entrepreneur, and motivator. Tragedy shifted the course of my life, but it also gave it a purpose-filled trajectory. I choose not to let adversity and hardship triumph over me; instead, I resolve each day to live with resilience.

About The Author

Tiran Jackson is a speaker, author, and entrepreneur that has used his tragic story about dealing with tragedy, loss, and overcoming as a means of helping others learn to overcome the setbacks that they encounter in their lives. After beginning his promising career as an engineer and living a life centered around advancing in his profession and providing for his family, he has gone through an incredible transformation, using his new, profound purpose as the means of inspiring others to find their path in life. Through his transformative journey, he has rediscovered who he is authentically and has allowed his vulnerability to serve as a guide in helping others find their resiliency, courage, and strength. He is inspiring those to move forward to reach their greatest dreams.

Learn more about him at RebornResilient.com

FIND THE STRENGTH WITHIN

For individuals, businesses, and organizations at a critical crossroads, or those looking for an inspired perspective to look within and rediscover the courage, strength, and clarity to overcome, visit RebornResilient.com to learn more.

Tiran Jackson provides the following services through the Reborn Resilient Platform:

- Virtual and In-Person Keynote Speaking Services (primarily centered on the following topics):
  - Resiliency in Times of Severe Adversity
  - Overcoming Trauma, Tragedy, and Dealing with Life-Altering Transition
  - How to Support Those in Your Care Facing a Tremendous Loss
  - Regaining Organizational Focus After Facing Major Setback
  - Finding and Addressing our Mental and Emotional Health After Life-Altering Loss
- Workshop Facilitation
- 1-on-1 Coaching : Life & Accountability / Trauma & Tragedy
- Group Coaching: Life & Accountability / Trauma & Tragedy
- Panel Discussions
- Podcast Interviews
- Online Education Programs

@RebornResilient

Reborn Resilient

Tiran Jackson

@tIran_jackson